GC

Tom Eadie

1st edition
published in 2011 by

Woodfield Publishing Ltd
Bognor Regis PO21 5EL England
www.woodfieldpublishing.co.uk

ISBN 1-84683-114-8

Printed and bound in England

Cover design: detail from a
self-portrait by Tom Eadie

Going Nowhere

A young man's experiences at home and abroad with the Royal Artillery in Malaya – 1946-57

TOM EADIE

Woodfield

Woodfield Publishing Ltd

Bognor Regis ~ West Sussex ~ England ~ PO21 5EL

tel 01243 821234 ~ **e/m** info@woodfieldpublishing.co.uk

Interesting and informative books on a variety of subjects

For full details of all our published titles, visit our website at

www.woodfieldpublishing.co.uk

The book is dedicated to my intransigently reticent, complicated, misunderstood, too often unappreciated, gloriously capable, and painfully frustrated late father, Charles William Eadie.

And to Maureen, my infinitely patient and indulgent wife of fifty-two years.

"Funny old buggers, us Welsh"

~ CONTENTS ~

Foreword .... *ii*

Introduction .... *iv*

1. Into The Valley 1990 1
2. Day in the Life 1946 11
3. In Deference To Heroes 1947 15
4. Umgawa and Others 1948 19
5. Earning and Learning 1951 25
6. Tortured by Technicolor 1954 31
7. Road to Tinker's Green 1954 49
8. Home Truths 1954 67
9. Summer and Suffering 1954 76
10. Autumn and Away 1954 84
11. Hong Kong 1955 98
12. Moving On 1955 116
13. Patrols, Holes and Food Checks 1955 134
14. Things to Do In Salak Bahru 1955 144
15. Causes and Effects 1955 155
16. Boh 1955/56 164
17. The Leaving 1956/57 172

Postscript: *182*

About the Author

Having been born in 1936 in the Swansea Valley and despite an early exile since 1938, I somehow instinctively retained far more subconscious Celtic influences than are perhaps either relevant or deserving, and which even now remain remarkably predominant, and infinitely rewarding.

From my father I inherited a instinctive inclination to demonstrate that circumstances are all too often a denial of ability.

My wartime education was unsurprisingly unspectacular, unrewarding, and largely resented, and left no recognisable result other than a regret that one's possible accomplishments were unfortunately completely ignored in the interests of traditional social expediency.

I was enlisted into the army in 1954 and served three years with the Royal Artillery in the UK, Hong Kong, and Malaya during the Communist Insurgency, an experience which I regard as having been perhaps fundamentally beneficial, but not particularly culturally reassuring.

Since enforced retirement, I have consciously attempted to develop my two great obsessions, painting and writing.

Preface

This project began in 1993 as a personal exercise in producing hopefully humorous but relevantly observed chapter length interpretations of specific points within the most formative part of my early life and at the same time helped clarify some of my family's hitherto unresearched genealogical ambiguity and was only later converted into book form, its eventual completion receiving a good deal of impetus as the result of a near fatal heart attack in 2007.

The book is primarily intended for those old enough to remember or interested in appreciating a time when existence appeared even more intimidating than it appears now but, with far more luck than judgement, a combination of minimal social pretence and an enforced appreciation of priorities, we endured a period when the problems which continue to confront society and defy solution first became intimidatingly apparent.

My intention in putting it together was simply to offer a reasonably accurate collection of personal memories and ironically humorous observations and interpretations of events and attitudes at a time in history which has often been dismissed as too dull and earnest to generate much nostalgia, not least by those who allow their assumption to be defined solely by meaningless superficial social comparisons and ignore completely its underlying significance.

It is also a rebuttal of the assumption that austerity necessarily indicates social monotony and that appreciable postwar transformation only really began during the 1960s, when in fact the inevitable, if avidly resisted (by the establishment) readjustment to attitudes and expectations actually developed much earlier.

It is also inevitably something of a personal lament for the fundamentally important standards which once seemed so indelibly a part of our existence and which now increasingly seem redundant. beneath the weight of overassertive individual expression.

Tom Eadie, 2011.

Introduction

It was in early 1992 during an holiday in West Wales with my wife Maureen, and my youngest surviving sister Lilian Maud, always referred to as Maudy and her husband Robert, never referred to as Bob, that my re-introduction and consequential fascination with the Swansea Valley began with our initial journey over the Black Mountain to find my birthplace, the oddly isolated mountainside village of Godre'r' Graig and from which developed a determination to research and record both the history of the area and my families association with it, and which has since provided a valuable source of material for my various writings.

1. Into the Valley, 1990

We made the winding ascent of the Black Mountain by car, watched by a few dismissive sheep grazing on pale rubble-littered grass among lumpy limestone outcrops, and having negotiated its convoluted route began the precarious descent to Upper Brynamman above deep gullied streams sparkling in the wake of undulating shadows, before drumming over a final cattle grid to roll past the villages of Rhosaman, Ystradowen and the two Cwm Twrchs down to Gurnos and the main A4067 road running along the base of the Swansea Valley.

I was in search of my birthplace, Hodgson Road, Godre'r Graig, to which my family incessantly referred; an insistently intrusive figment, the existence of which throughout my childhood had seemed completely anecdotal, as intangible an illusion as the court of King Arthur or the Sherwood lair of Robin Hood, though admittedly its very obscurity occasionally provided a welcome touch of agreeable distinction during schoolyard discussions in comparison to the more prosaic origins of most of my childhood companions.

Also, being of Welsh birthright, a characteristic dependent, admittedly, upon little more than a blissfully unaware first few months of life and residence, being hauled around, shawl-wrapped on the hip of my accommodating twelve-year-old sister, Lucy Florence, which initially induced a touchingly instinctive sense of national pride, although much later became somewhat diffused with the increasingly perplexing awareness of my family's actual genealogical ambiguity.

At what point in the history of that much-abused valley area the hamlet of Godre'r' Graig had first begun to string its eventual untidy ribbon of homes along that precipitous shelf on the south-western slope of Mynydd Allt-y-grug, between Ystalyfera and Pontardawe, is open to question, the road itself possibly having origins among the ancient West Glamorganshire droving and trade track-ways.

However, evidence of some habitation was already apparent when the first section of the canal pushed along the valley base from Swansea further to exploit the rapidly increasing industrialisation of the upper regions in 1796. At that point, it lay beside what was the primary route through the valley, a doubtlessly hazardous track probably already experiencing the occasional rock falls which were to eventually culminate in the modern A4067 valley-bottom highway being developed in response to the catastrophic landslips of the 1960s, when the village's north-eastern end collapsed to leave the foreshortened remains in their present sad state of elevated seclusion peering down at the traffic and silently negotiating the modern highway-covered route of the now largely obliterated sixteen-mile-long canal like some resentfully wounded pulpit-bound chapel preacher.

Upon our eventual arrival, the most evident access to the village required a sharp right turn from the main road, followed by a short climb up to the entrance of a single street, where, having parked the car, we sat amidst the gloomy light filtering through mardy-looking clouds, heavy with the threat of imminent rain, while I struggled to reconcile my own long-held illusions with the first sobering intrusion of disappointing reality, before leaving the car and failing miserably in an initial search to discover anywhere remotely identifiable as Hodgson Road, and in desperation enquiring of a passing girl as to its probable location, only to be met with an abrupt and adamant assertion that no such place existed anywhere in the village.

So I slouched back, completely bewildered, still trying to conceive some logical explanation, until a few moments later a small middle-aged man approached and waited patiently while being pressed with my plaintive enquiries.

"Duw, Duw, love," he responded.

"That street isn't here.

It was built a mile down the road, no room on the mountain see? Funny old buggers us Welsh, aren't we, building half a village somewhere else!"

After thanking him profusely, and elated with relief, I climbed back into the car to pass on the information to my companions.

We then drove hurriedly back down the incline to retrace our original approach until we saw, to the right and almost parallel with the rising road, the roofs of a line of buildings, and I swung the car to turn and cross a small culvert, to the wall of which was fastened a sign proclaiming 'Graig Newydd', and then turned again to pass a group of modern bungalows and enter a single street of semi-detached homes.

I parked the car halfway along its length to finally contemplate my precise birthplace, while my sister, the only one of my siblings not to have been born in South Wales, reacted to the rather run-down appearance of the area with all the misplaced pretension of someone now resident on one of the great faceless conurbations surrounding Birmingham by cowering in the back of the car and squealing, "Ooh, I wasn't born here!" while I struggled once more to accept the bewildering disparity between presupposition and truth.

Certainly, the street bore no resemblance to my 'How green was my valley' influenced adolescent imaginings of small stone cottages on grass-rich hillsides, this being simply two rows of quite impressively large homes erected in what must have been originally complete isolation on one of the few completely flat pieces of land in the area, the roadway itself being remarkably wide, and with each block seemingly endowed with sufficient contrast to its design and decoration to indicate that they had probably been eminently desirable homes when first erected in the 1920s.

So, after brusquely reminding my sister of her own origins in the less than impressive terraced 299 Gateford Road, Worksop, I climbed from the car once more and walked in the direction of where I presumed number 48 would be.

The street was completely deserted, but recognising I would be under close scrutiny from behind more than one set of front-room curtains, I tried to appear as nonchalant as possible and, having hurriedly taken a few photographs of my birthplace, returned to my companions.

This then was where my parents had eventually settled six years after the terrible dispute with my paternal grandfather over their enforced marriage in February 1921 and the prospective loss of my father's irreplaceable earnings as a young collier to a family of ten, at a time when the always volatile South Wales valleys were once again in turmoil at the prospect of the mines being handed back to private owners by an irresolute government evading its economic responsibilities at the end of the post-1914/18 war boom, being quite content to leave the confrontational owners to respond with their customary myopic insensitivity to instructions to reorganise the industry by introducing an immediate reduction in wages, and when faced with bitter opposition, the imposition of a total colliery lockout, during a year which has been described as one of the worst periods of economic depression since the Industrial Revolution.

Whatever the rights or wrongs of the cause of a family's feuds, and being only too aware of my father's considerable capacity for implacability, and probably by inference his father's also, it evokes little surprise that the situation could be so wilfully and obdurately left unresolved to bear the lamentable consequence of my father's future total alienation from his family, and remaining throughout his life so determinedly opposed to any suggestion of reconciliation, but sadly, also denying his children the knowledge and experience of a large part of the greater family for far too long.

However, it would also be unjust to interpret this as being necessarily indicative of a callous or insensitive nature, for that was never my father, and he was undeniably a far more complex individual than any of his children fully appreciated, certainly until far too late, his many hours spent in his own company working in his beloved greenhouse and garden or diligently accomplishing countless other tasks all resolutely directed towards the improvement or enhancement of our lot, which too often led to him being dismissed with the impetuosity of youthful conviction as being inherently moody, while selfishly accepting that we alone, to the point of obsession, would remain throughout his regrettably foreshortened life the one abiding concern upon which all other considerations rested, whilst those outside the family, who found themselves invariably frustrated by his taciturn demeanour, which most attributed to his being Welsh, which was actually an erroneous assumption, with father being no more Welsh than our mother! Although both spoke, Mother the most expansively, with sufficient traces of Celtic inflection to conceal their original dialects, which in the case of Father was Derbyshire and in the case of Mother Staffordshire.

Father was born in 1899 and raised until he was twelve years old in Chapel-en-le-Frith, where his father, Oliver Henry, moved in 1895 in pursuit of work as a railway employee, a detail of the family history which among so many remained obscured, largely through indifference, until I determined to research my ancestors fully and discovered that our origins lay far beyond the Swansea Valley or the Derbyshire Dales in the north-east of Scotland where our Great-great-great Grandfather William married Elizabeth Nicol and appeared as a bottle maker in South Leith in 1796.

Their second son, our Great-great Grandfather Thomas, moved to Dundee sometime before 1833, worked as a hairdresser and perfumer, and died in 1841, leaving his widow, Janet Fleming, with two sons aged seven and three, a daughter aged five, and pregnant with twins born just twenty days after their father's death, the surviving male twin being our Great Grandfather Oliver Gourlay Millar Eadie, who had moved to Perth with his English wife Aunt Eliza.

They then left Scotland for North Wales, but by 1875 were living in Weston-super-Mare in Somerset before moving to Newport, Monmouthshire in 1901.

Our Grandfather Oliver Henry moved from Derbyshire to Hereford in 1908, before settling in the Swansea Valley in 1911.

In contrast, Mother's family, the Bakers, seem to have ancestrally originated and evolved entirely within Kingswinford, a small industrial town on the outskirts of Dudley, until Thomas, my mother's father, moved his family into the Swansea Valley, presumably in pursuit of employment in his trade of bricklayer, possibly around the same period when the Eadies arrived and some eight decades before I sat in Hodgson Road trying desperately to create tangible images of my family's former existence from indistinct scraps of recollection and information assimilated and embellished throughout my childhood, and reluctantly acknowledging the impossibility of achieving anything approaching reasonable satisfaction.

It was of course all much too late, the changes wrought by the eclipse of the area's industrial past proving too great, the farms and fields and the sawmill passed by my brothers and sister on their journey to and from the infants and council school in the village long gone beneath bungalows and tarmac, the thirty-six-lock canal which, during that brief period before the arrival of the railways, ferried coal, iron, limestone and copper ore in the distinctive narrow-prowed boats and passed parallel with but above the level of Hodgson Road, having been gradually abandoned, and where it was not eventually filled and covered by the A4067 and left to trickle its dirty water through a tangle of invading undergrowth across the remains of a much foreshortened line of cottages, still bearing the enigmatically cryptic name of Chemical Row, while the steep slope above and beyond the raging River Tawe, itself now spanned by a sturdy steel bridge replacing the washed-away stone original across which the children had trooped to gather bilberries above the Swansea Vale section of railway, lay hideously naked with its ugly grey coating of accumulated spoil lacerated by horizontal track-ways and graffiti-adorned brick platforms of abandoned mine-pumping stations, and patiently awaiting the inevitable eventual covering of ash and birch trees slowly spreading up from the southern reaches of Craig y Fforest, but temporarily halted by a dearth of sub-soil.

The busy burnt umber waters of the stream, which spilled eagerly from beneath the culvert we had crossed at the rear of the street's gardens and into which, according to Mother, our father had once angrily complained, "Some wasteful bugger" had thrown loaves of precious bread, unaware they were in fact the results of an unsuccessful earlier attempt at baking by Mother, still sloppily jostled its way out towards the valley's northern towns.

Gone were the old historic hillside mines of Varteg, nicknamed 'Old Boot'; of Crimea, sunk from the opposite bank during the bitter winter of 1854 as an access shaft to the Ynysgeinon colliery when the canal froze for three weeks and prevented the miners from working; the Tereni/Gleison scene of the 1909 flooding disaster, when five men died and where my father worked, which was nicknamed 'Next week' in bitterly ironic recognition of its constant promise of possible future employment, when the big bell would be rung calling in the colliers, each pit now capped and forsaken with their tragic toll of sacrificed lives increasingly indistinct beneath the return of abundant woodlands, new roads, encroaching housing estates and growing public indifference.

The huge tin-plate works, brickworks, cloth factories, breweries and iron foundries, which once spewed smoke and pollution over the hillsides in contribution to the drizzle-grey sombre skies, which the non-Welsh so dismissively and mistakenly presumed epitomised the national character, all surgically removed, their foundations awaiting the interest of industrial archaeologists, the resulting flat areas occasionally transformed into manicured rugby and athletics fields, and the whole valley seemingly now in the process of at least physically drawing itself beyond the dismal evidence of its industrial past, and painfully and slowly reassuming the softer more colourful demeanour of its ancient agrarian tradition.

Even the cottage homes, which for so long had lined the valley's village streets in deep grime-layered, rain-streaked resignation, now increasingly gleamed, their walls bright with fresh paint, clean and proud of their utilitarian heritage, against a backdrop of revitalised hillside vegetation, at long last spared the old constant covering of dust and contamination.

Although oddly enough, Godre'r' Graig itself seemed to be one of the exceptions to this general impression of regeneration, perhaps due in part to its position of implied seclusion above the busy and more vegetative valley base, and to me, it unerringly conveyed a deep sense of melancholia with its high sadly foreshortened single street, which somehow left me with a wistful impression as to its significantly appropriate reflection in the personality of my father.

Between 1927 and 1937, Hodgson Road was my family's final home in the Swansea Valley, years in which governments came and went, each demonstrating little evidence of having assimilated much in the way of genuinely appreciated lessons from the industrial troubles following the First World War, and even less intention of implementing significant changes or solutions.

The old class divisions remained and were often exacerbated, and the old virulently bitter disputes continued, the most persistent inevitably concerning the miners and their wish for fundamental trade union rights, nationalisation and a national wages agreement, while the prosperous classes only too readily hypothesised as to the lower order's revolutionary intent, all of which persisted obstinately beyond the General Strike of 1926; that deplorably wasteful, ultimately avoidable event which had effected its most devastating retribution upon those areas least able to withstand its consequences, among which unsurprisingly were the South Wales coalfields.

Although regrettably my own knowledge of the family's actual day-to-day existence throughout this turbulent decade frustratingly consists of little more than a fragmentary assortment of snippets of recollected deprivation, bitter comments, observation and grumbling, primarily from Mother regarding governmental apathy as to the constant suffering, and a lingering resentful distaste for the involvement of one Winston Spencer Churchill, while the fact that my father had managed to move his growing family to the new council houses at Hodgson Road in 1927 – where a second son, Dennis Herbert, was born to join Oliver Charles born in 1921 at my maternal grandparents' home at Garden Cottage, Glantawe, in Ystradgynlais, and Lucy Florence born in 1924 at Goref Road – at a time when most miners felt sufficiently intimidated to resist attempting the realisation of any personal ambitions, must bear some tribute to his absolute determination, undoubtedly aided by Mother's considerable powers of persuasion, to provide the best available prospects for the future of the family.

In December 1930 a further son, Bert Alan, was born, with myself following in January 1936; to me, one of the most poignantly revealing details from this period is that, despite the apparent extensive acrimony caused by the rift that had occurred, the fact that my father agreed to name his first two children after his parents, and remained for seventeen years in close proximity to those who, under the circumstances, one might reasonably presume he would be most anxious to distance himself from at the earliest opportunity, must bear some indication of, or at the very least give hope of, a far greater depth of affection remaining than he was ever willing, or perhaps even capable of admitting to, and must beg the question of whether, aided by a little more induced incentive and a modicum of humility on all sides, a possible reconciliation could not at some point have been achieved.

But alas, this was not to be and as with most contentious disputes, logic was among the first and most abiding of casualties, though the prime cause of my father moving his family from the valley in 1937 was always earnestly interpreted to me as being for no other reason than the same universal sense of desperation resulting from continual disillusionment and lack of any foreseeable change in prospects that impelled thousands of other Welsh miners to abandon the valleys before the outbreak of the Second World War and resentfully move beyond their homeland.

Our retreat began with father obviously deciding to continue a long-practised family tradition and, irrespective of any sentimental attachments established throughout his twenty-seven years around Godre'r' Graig, or the fact that he was by then thirty-eight years old, being quite prepared to uproot and move to wherever in his opinion his family would be best served – which was initially Thurcroft in Derbyshire, the county of his birth, where he obtained lodgings, and two months later, having by then secured a rented house, sent for his family to join him.

We made the day-long journey crammed into a 'Mr Downes of Swansea' removal lorry, with Mother forever after claiming to have been infinitely unimpressed with Father's decision to abandon the valley, an opinion no doubt reinforced by the consequences of finding herself and her brood deposited in one of a street of hideous mining company-owned terraced hovels directly facing the colliery, a location which would always remain notoriously memorable as the coldest, dirtiest and most inhospitable place she was ever expected to set up home in, and even among my brothers as being so beset by draughts that the linoleum floor covering habitually rose knee-high whenever anyone opened a door.

The question of why, of all the available English mining areas he could have tried to obtain employment in at that time, my father happened to return to the county of his birth has never been satisfactorily answered, not least because, as with so much relating to my family, no one previously regarded it as of sufficient interest.

Certainly, the picturesque escarpment of the Combs Edge, Blue John, Speedwell and Peak Cavern part of West Derbyshire from which he originated was far more renowned for its limestone quarries than any coal mines, and having left the area as a boy of twelve it is difficult to imagine he would have been aware of the industrial make-up of the county's eastern area, where it borders the extensive South Yorkshire and North Nottinghamshire coalfields, so even without the benefit of defining evidence, it seems credible to assume that his return may well have been quite coincidental, while, despite Mother's assertion that he 'went looking for work', which implies it was purely speculative, the fact that the journey and obtaining of employment were accomplished together with two companions may, in contradiction, indicate that the journey was not conducted without some prior knowledge of prospects, and was perhaps made in response to an offer of recruitment.

2. Day in the Life, 1946

He halted, waiting momentarily before reaching up to release the latch on the front gate, looking towards the wide strip of stone-littered dry, dusty field where the rampant wild grasses, clover, dandelions and nettles that covered the surface of the remainder had long been removed by constant games with plank bats and rounded stones, the persistent pounding of hobnailed boots, grass fires ignited by broken milk bottles and the relentless excavation into the soft red sand of deeply-dug hideaways but, seeing no hint of activity, opened the heavy gate and stepped out, to pass the ever-present large, shallow pool of rainwater lying on the uneven surface of the short section of unfinished road.

As an eight year old, he appeared, as usual, no cleaner than he decided he needed to be, the long sleeves and buttoned-up collar of his rough jersey-hiding evidence of temporarily soap-and-water avoided parts, his hair tinged with auburn, bearing ample evidence of his father's home hairdressing kit, the greater part being shorn to the scalp, leaving only a short forehead fringe, his face rounded and with deep cheek dimples in his mother's likeness and his body, short, stocky and still bearing just sufficient adolescent plumpness for his older brothers, in their numerous less than considerate responses, to refer to him as 'Little Fat Nazi'.

At the beginning of the pavement, where the original street ended and the semi-detached block of No.46 and his own home at No.48 had been tacked on just prior to the outbreak of war, he looked directly across and noted the slight shiver of movement at the white lace curtain as Mrs Crisp at No.41 responded to her uncanny instinct for detecting the approach of anyone in short trousers and retained her customary position to defend the inviolable area of her front garden until danger had passed.

Mrs Hurst, wife of the bookies' manager, stepped from the gateless entrance of No.42 and almost collided with him, her two small, skinny daughters clinging to her skirt, their oversized eyes staring fearfully as he gave them the benefit of his best 'monkey face'.

At No.23 he halted his shuffling progress towards the bottom of the street, levered himself upwards and onto the wall-top and, having settled himself comfortably, turned his head to face the front window and gave out a long high-pitched whistle. The sound, ear-piercingly severe, vibrated around the walls and passageways of the closely packed street and startled enough of its over-population of dogs to provoke a staccato of howls and barks from end to end.

He smiled, satisfied with the resulting cacophony, as from the passageway a slightly-built boy in well-abused short trousers, collar-curling shirt and the remains of an undersized Fairisle jumper, blinked into the morning sunshine and grinned expansively, his pale face illuminated by the exposure of two rabbit-like front teeth, which protruded at an angle that lifted his top lip towards the base of his nose.

Silently but instinctively having decided their destination, the pair set off to wander to the end of the street, each with one foot on the 'corsey' edge and the other in the gutter in diligent search of anything remotely retrievable. Having, for once, been disappointingly unsuccessful, they then crossed to the other side and onto the small concrete forecourt of the corner shop to stand in a few moments of envious appreciation before the Fry's chocolate advert-adorned plate glass window and its interior display of large glass jars of diminishing stocks of pre-war confectionery, dusty boxes of patent medicines, jumbled hardware and fading cardboard promises of temporarily unredeemable advertising, before setting off once more to re-cross the street and follow the main road up past the sloping front gardens and shining white, uneven, limestone surface of the final street, nakedly awaiting the end of war and the eventual application of its tarmacadam coating, to eventually turn into the large gap beneath a wide-trunked, high oak tree beside the severe descent, which propelled the ancient turnpike road out past the unassuming jumble of stone cottages and farm buildings of the original hamlet of Gateford and overshadowed by the untidy hedgerow marking the boundary of their favourite haunt, the sand quarry.

The track beyond the large oak tree rose steadily, flanked to the left by the dilapidated garden fences, long-neglected privet hedges and a shoulder-high wide expanse of stinging nettles, and to the right, ending alarmingly abruptly where the noisy drag-line digger had gouged in to leave rouge-red vertical cliffs and create the high cone-shaped heaps of sand which dotted the low quarry area and pointed to the sky like a gigantic Red Indian encampment of tepees, encircled by winding track-ways, rivulets and occasional pools of crystal-clear water, which helped to create a landscape rich with possibilities for the only too avid imaginings of appreciative youngsters.

Lower down the turnpike road and opposite the small cottage, untidy barns and muddy stockyard of Gateford Farm, two large white-painted five-barred gates signalled the entrance to the quarry, a short distance inside which stood the imposing black corrugated shape of the loading shed. Here, the rich sand was dragged up the incline in squat steel tubs by way of a narrow tramway and then dumped into a large hopper, ready to be dropped into and await delivery from the always immaculate high-sided lorries, the procedure occasionally overseen by a dapper little foreman dressed, as befitted his position, in tweed jacket, collar and tie, heavy twill jodhpurs, boots and highly polished shin-length leather gaiters.

Beside the loading bay, the extent of the quarry halted abruptly before the sprawl of agricultural farmlands and here the high red banks rose just inside the line of the original hawthorn hedgerow and an occasional stunted oak, their top edges split by heavy rainwater run-offs and lower walls pocked at their most inaccessible levels with the deep dark entrance tunnels to sand martin nesting chambers, with the long cliff-line reaching across to the quarry's lateral limit to border the public footpath, which commenced at the top end of the final street and traversed away in the general direction of distant farms, hamlets and villages.

At the end of their stroll beside the garden boundaries, where the track ran in dizzying proximity to the highest point of the banks, the couple crouched, then tentatively lowered themselves to sit with short legs dangling over the abyss, fingers anxiously gripping the reassuring grass, each nervously aware of the precariousness and personal challenge implicit in his present position. They sat momentarily, unmoving, frozen in apprehension, until bravado prevailed and they relaxed enough to begin the animated, over-excited gabbling interposition of imaginings and interpretations only the juvenile mind can engender, while from the depths of a threadbare pocket a large chunk of gleaming 'pitch' was produced, broken, then shared and chewed with all the relish attributable to shop-bought confectionery. Having temporarily exhausted their excited participation in countless imaginary adventures among the gullies, streams and hillsides, they were up and off to round the corner, where the lumbering horse-drawn combine harvester was annually dragged through to salvage what little grain was produced in the wind-damaged, poacher-trodden, children-flattened field. Here they finally shuffled down the stubble slope and scrambled up the low bank directly behind their own street, before clambering onto the much-battered fence to sit like untidy gnomes and watch the 'backfield' cricketers bowl, bat and field to a set of rules unimagined by the MCC, while in the background the white walls of home glinted beneath the dark orange roof, its shared central chimney releasing an indolent curl of soft grey smoke from the 'damped-down' fire in the front room range up into the clean sharp light of early afternoon. At the end of the garden's long, heaped-up turf boundary wall, his father stooped, drove home and then lifted each heavy, heart-shaped shovel full of coal delivered by a flat-backed lorry into the house-end fuel store, his brilliantined, centre-parted, religiously rainwater-washed, slightly curling hair, impressively large ears and deep-lined features sweat-stuck with a thick, black coating of coaldust, which had begun its invidious invasion of his lungs the first day he had entered Tereni/Gleison pit as a fourteen-year-old boy.

3. In Deference to Heroes, 1947

By the time I reached my eleventh birthday, it was only too obvious, even to myself, that I was not one destined for any great mathematical eminence; indeed, concerning the area of mental arithmetic, I was continually struggling to assimilate much beyond its most basic principles at a time when it, above all other educational attributes, was continually emphasised as being a particularly essential accomplishment for anyone destined for the workplace, so unsurprisingly caused me some considerable distress and consternation, not least because to my chagrin, the cockeyed distribution of family genes had cruelly denied me any inheritance of my own mother's aptitude for that skill.

In all other educational subjects there was much less of a problem, while art always remained the one in which, had my world been a little different, I believe I may have achieved a reasonable enough degree of proficiency to perhaps have succeeded in elevating myself above the manual work, but did however at the time at least provide some sort of compensating personal confidence to help moderate my arithmetical misgivings.

To my abiding regret, and no doubt more than a little influenced by my numerical inadequacy, the memories I retain of my later school years seem to bear no little sense of antipathy generated by something akin to attendance of a Dickens-type academy, rather than any appreciation of comparable values to those portrayed in 'Goodbye Mr Chips', and certainly lack any memorable evocations of idyllic days filled with uniquely profound experiences or populated by extraordinarily influential tutors imparting their high ethical values and pronounced wisdom.

That is not to say that there were not some fundamentally competent teachers who laboured ceaselessly to sustain some semblance of however compromised standards during the final years of the Second World War and even after, but few found themselves with sufficient time, or were even encouraged by the system to proceed much beyond the parameters of the most fundamental instruction, or indeed anything requiring more than a minimal involvement in the continuation or encouragement of any pupil's progress.

There were of course some undeniably effective influences, but these, and certainly in my case, all too often tended to be of a rather negative nature, and on the odd occasion were rendered quite unpleasantly unforgettable by involving some sort of minor physical assault, with one unfortunate experience, to which I have always attributed at least some of the potential origins of my habitual antipathy and mistrust of most forms of authority taking place predictably during one of my dreaded torturously painful maths lessons, which on this occasion was being conducted by a young male temporary teacher who, having noticeably unsympathetically detected my faltering and embarrassed efforts to contend with a fractional exercise, and having as a consequence already contemptuously contributed to my increasing state of confusion and discomfort with sarcastic references as to the imperfection of my mentality, suddenly decided to compound my misery by ordering me to leave my position at the desk to stand before the entire class, an instruction which immediately seemed to me to constitute little more than a direction towards obvious public humiliation, and a spectacle to which I was not about to subject myself for anyone; so I refused to move, whereupon he immediately thundered down upon me and lunged to grab my shoulders and begin a furious attempt to physically drag me away from my seat, while I grimly resisted by clinging desperately to any available part of the heavy desk, while those fellow pupils seated alongside me retreated diplomatically, or fearfully, to the farthest end of the bench seat, and at least helped to provide a well-weighted anchor to my determined resistance, while the young teacher, being at this stage apparently in imminent danger of compromising his masculinity, responded by delivering several vigorous slaps to my head, and then locked his large hands on my wrists and eventually broke my grip by sheer force, resulting in both of us collapsing backwards and clattering to the floor in an undignified heap, at precisely the point at which the headmaster, having been alerted to the melee, entered the classroom.

I of course was immediately sternly directed to his study, convinced that I was about to receive the usual perfunctory hearing followed by one of his enthusiastically applied long bamboo cane wackings, but to my total bewilderment found myself on this occasion standing before his large mahogany desk being solicitously encouraged to relate my own version of events, and was actually listened to sympathetically before being instructed to return to the classroom, which by then was under the supervision of one of the regular teachers.

Later, I was recalled to the headmaster's study, still dubious as to my fate, but was once more treated with what by then seemed to me to be a rather suspiciously overweening degree of consideration, the reason for which however became abundantly clear when it was confirmed that the teacher involved had accepted that his unprofessional loss of control had been largely responsible for exacerbating the confrontation, but that as the lapse was the result of the stress and near mental breakdown he had suffered after his experiences during the war as a RAF fighter pilot, it would perhaps be advantageous to everyone if I were to agree to disregard the whole incident.

Now how much of this explanation was actually true I had no way of establishing, but to an eleven year old who, in keeping with most of his generation, regarded the Battle of Britain and its RAF heroes with a sense of awe bordering on total worship, and to whom a little scuffle and a few bangs to the head hardly constituted a particularly unique secondary modern school educational experience, I recognised that some situations, even if they could be construed as bearing very little personal guilt, can become ridiculously complicated with perpetuation and are often best left to fade into obscurity.

I did however, even at that early age, also appreciate that the motivation behind my remarkably benevolent treatment by our usually fiercely unsympathetic headmaster had far more to do with attempting to avoid any adverse reaction from my parents and his superiors than any genuine demonstration of equity or consideration for my welfare.

So the erring teacher duly and diplomatically disappeared from the school staff and the little episode quickly faded into insignificance, yet forever remained with me as a salutary lesson as to the absolute need, if necessary, to meet head-on whatever provocation I encountered, and the less edifying recognition that the retention of personal integrity and self-respect would, in the big dark world of adulthood, require rather more than implicit truth.

4. Umgawa and Others, 1948

Almost directly opposite the end of the street, the name association of which would eventually so offend the unsuspected sensibilities of its landlord that he changed it while still remaining more than willing to receive the rents, a gap in the long line of the main road houses signified the entrance to the establishment which was invariably referred to locally as the 'Bevin Huts', even though their original construction and designation as accommodation for a proposed five hundred of 'Big Ernie's' reluctant wartime mining conscripts had, by 1947, been developed and expanded with the ever-increasing numbers of prisoners of war and displaced persons, arriving to a point where its low-hutted sprawl provided a far better standard of facilities for a succession of Italians, Hungarians, Poles and Ukrainians than those endured by the majority of the surrounding civilian households, with its conveniently available labour being only too happy to supplement the seriously depleted workforce of the local coal mines, farms and industries rather than face the desolation of a Europe blistering with political uncertainty and industrial wreckage.

Little of the underlying political purpose for the camp's presence, or indeed even the reasons for the occasional changes to its always interestingly alien occupiers, seemed to play any significant part in the majority of the local populace's acceptance of its existence, or after each short period of initial mutual orientation seemed to unduly influence their readiness to participate in any available opportunity to fraternise with the inmates, provided of course this generosity of spirit was suitably reciprocated and the parameters of coexistence stopped short of discovering that someone's wife or daughter had actually taken up overnight residence within the camp.

Indeed, the level of tolerance and peaceful coexistence seemed to remain impressively high in a neighbourhood presumably no less affected by recent positively encouraged prejudices than any other gorged on the once apparent essentiality of wartime propaganda, though to what extent this situation was indirectly or otherwise deliberately influenced or manipulated by officialdom to minimise any possible conflict between the parties is impossible to ascertain, but there can be little doubt that the fundamental contributing factor was a sincere desire on the part of most people in the area to simply get on with attempting to reconstruct some sort of acceptable quality of life amidst the stringent economic impositions of early peace, and if that required a necessity to peacefully coexist with whosoever was presumably temporarily planted within their midst, then so be it.

Naturally, one of the most effective components towards maintaining the equilibrium of this state of détente was the camp's readiness and ability to provide facilities for a degree of live entertainment, which had almost totally disappeared under the more pressing considerations of wartime priorities, and its compact theatre soon became the venue for numerous concerts and shows, most of which seemed to involve the accompaniment of the piano-playing virtuosity of the white-haired manageress of the much-cluttered corner shop opposite the entrance to the camp, whose particular playing technique included a memorably graceful tendency to over-elaborate the height at which her hands rose above the keyboard, as if even the rendition of 'My Old Man Says Follow the Van' or 'Knees Up, Mother Brown' required the same dramatic emphasis as the 'Warsaw Concerto', while another constant and essential participant in the avidly attended entertainments at the little theatre was the local professional ventriloquist, who performed with his splendid dolls throughout the war and was also particularly active in organising the big VE and VJ day street parties and attendant fairground activities on the big 'Backfield', where the huge bonfires, which had been zealously guarded day and night by parents determined to prevent the neighbouring street's notorious gang of mini Impis, led by a grubby girl in ill-fitting boots, from conducting one of their periodic dustbin-lid-shield and house-brick-armed rampages to ransack or ignite them in advance, were at last lit and roared violently into the evening sky, showering arcs of brilliant orange sparks across the field to the severely startling accompaniment of illegally-acquired military thunderflashes and a few rather less forceful Jumping Jack and Catherine Wheel fireworks, while the occasional panicky adult dashed about, beating out the ensuing grassfires with an old coat, and we adolescent inheritors of post-war optimism, with blaze-reddened faces, sticky with sweat, hair reechy with oil-smelling smuts and clothes reeking like charcoal burners, rolled huge potatoes to roast among the bonfire's embers and squinted happily into the hypnotic inferno, oblivious to any assumed possible symbolic significance to our future.

Of course, any local public performance at that time would unavoidably include someone's bony little lovely clattering onto the stage in her prize possessions, a pair of big, black, patent-leather tap-dancing shoes, plated with enough steel to virtually guarantee perpetual balance and deprive some soldier of half his helmet, resplendent in a sacrificed, much-modified pre-war wedding gown and diligently watched over by her enraptured mother stage left, defiantly daring the audience to deny her perspiring purple-faced protégé anything less than absolute adulation as she proceeded to energetically bang away at some excruciating, unrecognisable interpretation of a Shirley Temple or Margaret O'Brian routine.

Supporting acts, as befitted their less illustrious ability, would range from a couple of school friends, convinced that the way to show business immortality lay in deliciously politically incorrect burnt cork blackened faces and singing painfully off-key versions of 'Mammy' and 'Camptown Races', or a pint-sized junior Max Miller with an embarrassingly cocksure attitude and a few, usually cocked-up recited jokes, while it remains to this day difficult to comprehend what, other than some distorted sense of aggression, compelled even brothers to enthusiastically climb into some tatty boxing ring at any gymkhana, church garden fête or sports day and proceed to ferociously clout black eyes and blood out of each other in the questionably justified pursuit of demonstrating the 'noble art', while refereed by a broken-nosed, cauliflower-eared past punch bag from the pre-war boxing booths or some big-bellied boozer in precarious trousers, dubious vest and ancient plimsolls, whose usual experience inside any type of ring was confined to the one situated at a disused quarry, where the local gamblers tossed coins every Sunday morning.

Cinema, of course, would remain the most consistent and lasting influential area of entertainment to our generation, right from those earliest incomparably precious farthing entrance fee sessions in a neighbouring back garden's large Nissen hut, fidgeting on beer-crate-supported plank seats under unsteady 16mm projections of the silent classics of Chaplin, Keaton and Turpin, to the post-war Saturday morning matinee anarchy in the town's picture houses prior to exuberant participation in the unimaginatively repetitive adventures of enumerable Western heroes in impeccable and impressively tight-trouser Hollywood-designed outfits who, inevitably and annoyingly, broke into embarrassingly soppy songs about horses and the wide open spaces to Peroxide-blonde cowgirls the moment the Los Angeles studio set and location shot range were cleared of any inconvenient redskins, or some pack of snarling hangers-on led by a black Stetson-wearing villain who had been bloodlessly despatched by ivory-handled six-shooters with a perplexing inability to recognise their own ammunition capacity.

Whilst no world war conditioned hero-susceptible youngster could be expected to resist the savagely hazardous exploits of a loin-clothed ape man, with an exhilarating if physically impossible vocal yodel accompanied by a slightly bonkers chimpanzee, magisterially free to combat the persistent incursions into his Bel-Air back-lot jungle by safari suited European hunters treacherously assisted by scary witch doctors draped in tiger skin and blacked-up midgets uttering screen writers' mumbo jumbo, as he led hordes of elephants in artificial ears who responded universally to the single command of "Umgawa!" and applauded by companies of extras in ape costumes, superhumanly wrestled huge rubber crocodiles and returned his liana and bamboo mod-con treetop des res back once more to its idealistic state of great American dream naivety, or even fail as a thirteen year old to be profoundly inspired by a Mickey Rooney 140 mile an hour back-projected drive in the Indianapolis 500 motor race wearing a polo helmet, a pair of goggles and an Hawaiian-style short-sleeved shirt to finish in third place in a flame-engulfed car, and then be presented with first prize by the admiring actual winner.

Later of course, the cinema and we 'grew up', and the old naive illusory standards were no longer fashionable or therefore appropriate; 'progress' and its assumed sophistication had fuelled an acceptance of greater and more realistic cinematic violence until what we were watching, still presumably as some sort of muddled escapism, became infinitely more confusing than reality, and we, intoxicated with the misapprehension that someone was at last paying our generation heed, accepted its eternally posturing, ominously mentally confusing, self-centred anti-heroes with a degree of pertinence to our own situation, which appears in retrospect unjustifiably presumptive and arguably hardly positively contributive to our future composure.

Although at least the emerging crop of younger heroines provided a welcome and more appropriate alternative to the now diminishing appeal of most of the older female film stars, even if rather disconcerting for red-blooded young men with raging hormones to see beauties like Janet Leigh, Natalie Wood, Jean Peters, Piper Laurie and Pier Angeli all too often romantically paired with ageing and physically disintegrating male leads, who unerringly revealed that they were egocentric enough to actually believe the union was entirely conventional, while we, the unsure, uncouth youth of a disorientated nation greeted Toni-permed, bright cotton-print dressed, white-gloved girlfriends with commendable old-fashioned courtesy as they alighted with severely tested grace from the unstable bottom steps of incoming buses, and in once-weekly pressed gabardine suits and with arm-draped neatly folded raincoats escorted them to the back rows of fading glory, audience-dwindling cinemas in the few propitious remaining days before the surviving local picture houses were finally subjected to the wretched indignity of staging Syncopating Sandy piano-playing marathons, and television increasingly implanted its insidious enticement into the sanctity of the front parlour.

Of course, radio had also played a significant role in our entertainment, particularly during those snow-deep, dark freezing winter evenings when the prospect of ice-numbed raw and chapped sock covered fingers and rubber Wellington boot inflicted stingingly sore red-ringed legs provided a far less tempting alternative to perching on one of mother's utility dining chairs in the suffocating heat of our overpopulated front room, earnestly awaiting the dramatic musical introductions to the latest edition of *Dick*

Barton, Special Agent or the detective tales of *Paul Temple*, and developing a lifelong appreciation of the imaginatively loony creations of Tommy Handley, Richard Murdoch and Jimmy Edwards together with my mother and father, who venerated the radio or the 'wireless' with an almost evangelical regard and always insisted upon owning, irrespective of cost, the best possible receiver, which, in his implacable opinion, meant none other than the latest model produced by British manufacturers Pye or Cossor, preferably one elegantly cased in a burnished mahogany cabinet, upon which he could indulge his penchant for polishing to a mirror-like finish every inch of its surface, for he, who spent so great a part of his life in the deep, dirty featureless darkness of pit bottoms, always found the infinite organic complexities of wood grain a compelling fascination.

The *Armchair Mysteries, The Man in Black, Saturday Night Theatre* – all these and numerous others filled many an uncomplicated hour of our lives, in an age when time, its passage and the compulsive insistence as to its maximal productive use seemed to be so much less of a preoccupation, and the pleasantly unpretentious unsophisticated nature of countless variety and popular music shows unfailingly lifted us blissfully into those much-appreciated diversions of intellectually undemanding enjoyment, which so effectively imparted such indelible memories and exasperated the zealous crusading of those persistently vocal paragons of public taste ever eager to impose upon the majority their own definition of cultural amelioration.

5. Earning and Learning, 1951

In January 1951 I, along with many other positively relieved fifteen-year-old boys, joyfully abandoned the brown linoleum-floored interior of our back street grey-stone box-like school, leaving its penknife-engraved, ink-tattooed heavy desks and dog-eared reference books to our succeeding crop of combatants and, pathetically unprepared, blundered out beyond the insulation of adolescence into the impoverished perplexity of a year of meat shortages, a fuel crisis and a flu epidemic, and each weekday morning rose at five a.m. to leave home equipped with an ex-army gas mask bag containing a bottle of cold sugar and milk-less tea and six slices of bread and jam wrapped in newspaper, and together with half a dozen other ex-St John's Boys School recruited friends cycled the six miles beyond the edge of town as employees of the Forestry Commission in the 420 acres of Whitwell Wood, which was as close as someone of my overactive imagination and non-existent resources could realistically envisage becoming one of the hundreds of prospective immigrants daily besieging the Canadian Embassy and actually becoming a lumberjack in the giant redwood forests of British Columbia.

Naturally, the demands of a job which never seemed to expect more of us than trimming the dead lower branches from dense plantations of Scots pine, clearing scrub hazel or chopping down plenty of silver birch and the occasional slimy sycamore, or struggling to control the inclinations of a large-wheeled, lethal-looking grass cutter between rows of newly planted ash and oak, while watching for panic-stricken noisily rising pheasants abandoning hoards of much-prized pale brown eggs, proved ideally suited to our constant immature need to reiterate our physicality.

Unlike the daunting prospect of substituting one set of classrooms and teachers for another contemplated by those among our age group in a position to attend the local technical college as trade apprentices, we were resignedly unconcerned with attempting to move beyond the parameters of our traditional manual non-commitment, naively convinced that we were as near to being our own masters as our position would allow, did our work, went home, paid for our lodging, drank Black and Tan beer in the back rooms of accommodating public houses, smoked heavily, convinced of its masculinity, clumsily and self-consciously propelled 4711 cologne perfumed shop assistants and factory girls around the darkened interiors of the local dancehalls, and determinedly disregarded any point in time beyond the next seven days.

Whitwell Wood, where most of our time was spent, had at the centre of its wheel-like layout a large clearing on which stood a huge corrugated-metal sheet cabin, where we reported each morning to receive our orders for the day, and also retired to and maintained our tools when the weather was too wet.

The cabin was accessed from the main road by a wide fire-break driveway, the total area of the plantation being divided into smaller fire-break pathways radiating from the centre like spokes, which ended at the outer limits before a wire mesh, supposedly rabbit-proof, perimeter fence.

The Forestry Commission was at that time one of the largest employers and, provided one was prepared to accept that it could never offer comparable wages to coal mining, did however provide a much healthier and more relaxed working environment, and for the next couple of years our little band were content to wander the luxuriant quiet acres of oak, elm, pine, beech and birch, happily unfettered by clocking systems or very much in the way of direct supervision, just occasionally being called upon to destroy large wasp nests with a stick dipped in a tin of cyanide paste, causing hilariously observed mayhem among the members of the local fox hunt, as they big-arsed and self-importantly thundered up and down the driveways before we bolted the occasional mount with an accurately catapulted stone directed from the cover of the plantation, or harassed amorous horizontal couples from passing cycle clubs availing themselves of the undergrowth by creeping up and pulling off the covering oilskin cape, before galloping away in fits of laughter, usually pursued in hopeless desperation by the red-faced, violently swearing boyfriend clutching his unbuttoned shorts.

Some mornings, we smuggled in a dismantled 22 rifle like some Mafia hit man, and with the assistance of two ferrets inexpertly hunted rabbits on the slopes of a small magnesian limestone gorge, which dropped dramatically beyond the eastern limit of the plantation, or diligently erected garrotte snares or 'snickels', their loops supported by carefully fashioned hazel wood 'pricker pegs' at any point where the chicken wire boundary fence had been breached, a practice which rather lost its appeal after it resulted in one companion removing the ends of three fingers of his left hand during a less than attentive attempt to trim the end of a peg with a grass sickle.

Accidents such as this, during that safety regulation untrammelled age, were in retrospect unsurprisingly rather more prevalent than appreciated at the time, the always competitive pursuance of acquiring an exceedingly sharp, blithely unrecognised, potentially lethal combination, which resulted in the occasional blade embedding itself in someone's arm or leg, and the sobering prospect of a panic-stricken dash to the nearest habitation to find a telephone, if available, and a trip to hospital in the General Manager's sleek Armstrong Siddeley, struggling to keep blood off the shiny leather upholstery, or in desperation, a frantic race with the victim being carried on someone's back.

The unfortunate accidents aside, it was on the whole however a remarkably carefree introduction to the world of work for a young man, and provided we completed to a reasonable standard our daily requirement of keeping the woodlands in a presentable state, no one bothered us unduly, with the exception of an occasional irritating interference from an overly officious ancient who lived in a bungalow at the wood's entrance, who being himself a Commission employee seemed to assume his longevity entitled him to qualification as some sort of unofficial supervisor and consequently the main conveyor of mischievous tales of our youthful shortcomings to our occasionally visiting area manager, a gentleman undeservedly endowed with the name of Bill Thick, who thankfully was always rather more inclined to an appreciation of the old man's buxom daughter than a serious reaction to any resentfully vindictive stories, and seemed largely prepared to let us disappear into the woodland's wide acres like the last of the Mohicans to explore the many tracks and trails and generally indulge ourselves with much the same degree of freedom and doing much the same things we had enjoyed before leaving school.

Of course, we all recognised and accepted, with a remarkable complaisance, that all this was very much a temporary and transitory state of affairs, the inevitability of National Service hovering just over the horizon being something no one could ignore completely, even if most of our like were quietly determined within our submissive conformity to enjoy our temporary freedom while disregarding any possible indulgence in pointless protests; we were after all, being one of the last generations born before the Second World War, rather too well programmed for that, and accepted and reflected relatively unquestioningly the moral and social dictates of our elders.

While there is a great deal of evidence to suggest the initial germination of the great readjustments to attitudes and approaches resulting in today's excessively abused and often questionably beneficial freedoms originally lay within those early post-war years, any significantly effective expression of discontent was at the time utterly beyond our comprehension, and would require a further decade of development, fuelled by a large injection of materialism, before its eventual manifestation.

By the time I approached my seventeenth birthday I was growing increasingly dissatisfied with the fact that much less of our time was being spent in the local woods and more and more out in the great flat featureless wilds of Lound to the north of Worksop, where we endured long uneventful days planting mile upon mile of conifers, and so I decided that this would be an opportune time to undertake a change of employment, not with any overwhelming intent to acquire a more fulfilling or long-term advantageous career, which, had it even entered my head, would have been pointless at that juncture, but primarily as a means of hopefully improving my financial status before the War Office came calling.

So I made the move into the most easily available and potentially lucrative alternative, the building trade, which at the time was beginning to enjoy a period of enormous expansion, with housing schemes being rushed through by local councils with almost lackadaisical rapidity and with large contracts being doled out with gay abandon in a desperate effort to address the dearth of accommodation created by the war, and resulting, a time long before the blandishments of huge construction companies proved to be of irresistible attraction to susceptible council officials, in local contracts being awarded to local companies who cannily met the national lack of skilled tradesmen by exploitatively entrusting the completion of such contracts to an overwhelming percentage of apprentice craftsmen.

So I became a general labourer, first as a banks-man assistant to a Ruston-Bucyrus mechanical excavator driver, an occupation which basically required me to stand around with misplaced self-importance holding a cross-shaped sight board as the machine's huge bucket gouged out the deep mains services trenches, and periodically helping to hand-pump fifty-gallon drums of diesel into the eternally thirsty monster, and being ferried to and from work each day clinging on for dear life as a fraudulently nonchalant pillion passenger behind the slightly barmy digger driver, who recognised only top gear and no speed limits on his 500cc AJS motorcycle.

With the drainage excavations completed, I moved on to suffer as an initially struggling member of a concrete gang constantly ferrying heavy steel wheelbarrows brim-filled with sloppy concrete from the rumbling mixers to the latest set of foundations, where a perpetually complaining, sarcastically offensive sixteen-stone misery was responsible for laying the final rafts, and I, after sweating and puffing over site rubble and narrow pathways with every inexperienced arm, leg and stomach sinew and muscle aching, balanced and forced an unstable barrow up an inclined scaffolder's board before making the final supreme effort of raising the handles, driven purely by sheer determination and fear of losing face, to dump the already settling contents ready for dispersal.

Thankfully, things got easier with repetition and, being always psychologically incapable of turning the other cheek to any personally directed antagonism, I derived a great deal of satisfaction later with the ability to accurately time and judge the disposal of the barrow contents so that they flooded around the ankles of the big fat moaner before nonchalantly strolling away, leaving him to his red-faced clumsy efforts to extricate his embedded Wellington boots while howling at me in a state of near apoplexy, threatening reprisals ranging from broken legs to buggery.

With most of the concrete gang being rather older than me, one of the things that I, as a not obsessively money-orientated individual, soon became aware of and constantly disliked was the surprising degree of jealousy, vindictiveness and downright hostility generated among those of my more supposedly mature companions, whom I mistakenly presumed would have been inclined to a rather more tolerant attitude towards each other, whenever any question related to wages, bonus or overtime was raised, so I was more than happy to eventually get the opportunity to leave them to their grown-up money-grubbing little feuds and move to the bricklaying gangs as a labourer among people of my own age, the apprentices, and to find myself among people of whom the majority had thankfully not yet succumbed to total avarice, and who were even quite prepared to help me through the first fraught couple of weeks when I struggled to keep pace with supplying them adequately with bricks and mortar, so it came as no surprise to find that I soon developed many long-lasting friendships and spent a great deal of memorably enjoyable time in their company away from the building site drinking, socialising and doing the very ordinary things which to today's rather more sybaritically excessive young would no doubt seem unutterably unexciting and unspeakably boring, but to me have always retained a particular touch of poignancy to a period of my life when the mundane content was more than compensated by the degree and quality of the companionship it conferred.

6. Tortured by Technicolor, 1954

I suppose with a social content defined by American Atom bomb tests at Bikini Atoll, the defeat of the French army at Dien Bien Phu and persistent promises of eternal salvation from ex Fuller Brush salesman Billy Graham, 1954 could never lay claim to being one of the more celebratory periods in history, reasonably representative of its unpredictable decade perhaps, and even occasionally indicating that we as a nation were at last emerging from the post-war austerity so exacerbated by the vindictive reactions of a socialist-scared America to the Labour Party's election victory in 1945.

Food rationing was finally fried into folklore, the remaining constraints on meat, bacon and butter belatedly recognised as indefensible in an economic merry-go-round that saw large parts of the total tax revenue constantly squandered in attempts to develop repeatedly outmoded atomic weapons, while our industrial and social infrastructure still exhibited more acres of weed-covered bomb damage than any convincing evidence of recovery.

Industry still retained high levels of labour, so employment was plentiful, though its availability perversely helped to precipitate the class-directed mistrust and retribution that left us beset with strikes and go-slows, evermore desperately short of essentials, and up to the White Cliffs of Dover in national debt, while throughout it all we continued to be tortured by Technicolor images of American affluence, crucified by excessive American war loan commitments and irritated by the generous American investments in the two nations we had bankrupted our national assets, primarily to America, in trying to defeat a painfully ludicrous situation, which would have been all the more remarkable had it resulted in anything other than a good deal of the population appearing uninspired, unmotivated and conditioned to expect little more from the foreseeable future than a prolonged wait for a council house or, in desperation, a ten-pound assisted passage to some Australian sheep station.

On the other hand, being still the products of antiquated social and educational systems, which had the greatest difficulty in recognising and accepting the changes demanded by the advent of the nuclear age, we ingenuously expected to affect 'morally correct' solutions to an increasingly immoral world's problems, and faced each loony lurch into the terrifyingly uncertain future with never more unconvincingly stiff upper lips, while being ineffectually exhorted to evoke the 'Dunkirk spirit' by the same bunch of pseudo patriots who had so quickly and quietly removed their responsibilities from our beleaguered realm before the first little boat left harbour in 1940.

However, we had at least received some acknowledgement for the previous twelve years of sacrifice when we were invited to gape at the Festival of Britain in 1951, but even that inspired exercise in exhibiting the largely unobtainable and eminently unaffordable, proved somewhat indicative of our indeterminate prospects by being hurriedly torn down by the petulant incoming Tory government, to the delight of the scrap men and the excited anticipation of those individuals awaiting an opportunity to purchase one of the aluminium ashtrays recycled from its most pointed and pointless exhibit, the Skylon.

Inevitably, it would be that thankfully interminably unpredictable element, youth, which would eventually manifest the initial opposition to the unquestioning conformity upon which the establishment so depended and piously presumed was their right to expect, and stimulated by, or reflected in, a sometimes questionably sincere artistic advocacy, would finally initiate the sea change which committed society's traditional imbalance to historical mythology, and actuate, rightly or wrongly, the eventual pursuit of individuality.

Of course, if you happened to be male and fortunate enough to reach your eighteenth year with reasonably formed feet and both eardrums intact, and had avoided succumbing to Tuberculosis or Poliomyelitis, the odds were that any serious hopes of pursuing outrageous concepts such as individuality would be temporarily relinquished, and all responsibility regarding the immediate future presented to the one government department not exactly renowned for its ability to ensure anyone's welfare, the War Office, a prospect anticipated by most young men with a mixture of considerable resentment and apprehension, and by myself in particular with an initial regret that my dear father, in his adamantine wisdom, had seen fit to forbid the possibility of my escaping into the ever open arms of the National Coal Board, which along with servitude to some local farmer, most of whom still operated under practices and conditions indicative of the books of Thomas Hardy, was one of the few legal alternatives to military conscription open to anyone denied the convenience of a trade apprenticeship, and one that afforded me the opportunity of a long bus ride down the Great North Road to Nottingham in full sartorial splendour of semi-drape jacket, narrow-legged trousers, yellow socks, crepe-soled shoes and an ex Merchant Navy raincoat, which was a personal compromise on an unaffordable Humphrey Bogart-type trench coat and a well Sylvikrinned hairstyle heavily influenced by Tony Curtis, to lounge my way into the central bus station under cover of a North Nott's pea-soup fog, which had obviously left the banks of the River Trent for no other reason than to aggravate my increasingly nervous disposition, and to someone more accustomed to negotiating ploughed fields and building sites than intimidating dense city backstreets presented a challenge, which left me shivering in the station café, desperately begging directions from any passing bus driver, clippie and the lady who cleaned the tables.

However, after a couple of cups of tea and several nervously hurried cigarettes, the poisonous murk thinned just enough to raise my hopes of making an escape, and at appointment time, and an irrational conviction that a late arrival would possibly result in my immediate imprisonment for desertion, I crept out of the station area, and with the occasional assistance of the pavement edge as a general guide managed to blunder my way out into the surrounding streets where, with frantic appeals to one or two startled passer-by, and as a consequence of more than one perambulation of the same stretch of roadway, I eventually arrived at my destination, damp and cold, but triumphantly relieved to enter a miserably insignificant building to present my official invitation to a thin-faced unhappy-looking lady receptionist continually struggling to communicate from behind an almost permanently positioned handkerchief soaking up the symptoms of a heavy head cold, and who, after much deliberation and obvious irritation over the spelling of my place of birth, directed me to a small waiting room already occupied by several other less than enthusiastic candidates, most of whom seemed to be seriously intent upon committing eventual hara-kiri by replacing the already inadequate supply of oxygen with a thick mixture of Woodbine and Old Holborn cigarette and pipe smoke while indulging in one of our time-honoured social charades, that of not visibly acknowledging that anyone else was actually present in the room.

Two hours later, and having in the meantime watched surreptitiously with sympathy from the farthest point from anyone else I could manage as half a dozen preceding victims shuffled dejectedly out in response to a summons from a self-important little Hitler with a clipboard and wearing a suit that had probably first graced his grandfather, he reappeared once more to this time call out "Eddie!" which I took to be one of the less imaginative mispronunciations of my surname, and having received in return for my temerity in voicing a correction the sort of piteously dismissive look favoured by such higher-intellect beings when confronted by ill-bred idiots with unpronounceable names, I plodded out behind him down a short corridor to be ushered deferentially into the presence of a large florid-faced gentleman dressed in tweed-plus-fours and a matching waistcoat bulging beneath an unbuttoned, once white overall, who grumpily ordered me, in a voice obviously accustomed to being instantly obeyed, to "Remove all clothing, including undergarments, if applicable," which in my case certainly was not, I being of the no vest, underpants and where necessary hiding any holes in my socks with the occasional discreet fold end of the social scale, while my dawdling self-conscious strip hardly endeared me to him or possibly helped his blood pressure as he bellowed, "Come on, boy, get a bloody move on; no one's the slightest bit interested in your inadequate appendages!" before proceeding to poke, prod and press where no one else had gone before in what seemed to be a questionably indulgent attempt to ascertain whatever can be ascertained from the less appealing areas of human anatomy, before abruptly and just as grumpily ordering me to take up my discarded clothing and directing me towards the next room and a second reincarnation of Dr Mengele, who seemed inexplicably interested in collecting a sample of the urinary bi-product of the two cups of tea I'd consumed back at the bus station café, which he studiously re-brewed over a small gas burner.

Having presumably failed to detect any cause to despatch me direct to Nottingham General Hospital, he pointed me in the direction of the next humiliation and so the long embarrassing morning progressed, with me shivering into each examination in a state of acute apprehension, then hurriedly stumbling out again, clutching my crumpled clothing and experiencing an all too brief rush of relief when it was all over, and having thankfully regained some semblance of dignity in re-dressing, I departed the building with an even greater sense of urgency than when I had entered and bolted back up the Great North Road, musing resentfully over the prospect of devoting the next phase of my short life to probably protecting the interests of people who regarded those of my background as about as much use as an empty uniform, and spending the interim period awaiting the arrival of the next OHMS communication, putting as they say, my affairs in order, an undertaking which actually amounted to little more than parting with my adored racing pigeons, paying off the hire purchase on my big Rudge bicycle and being unceremoniously dumped by my current girlfriend as a result of a Sunday tea summons from her mother, a charmingly polite lady who aspired to some small literary recognition by composing rhyming tales about elves and fairies, and upon whose worthy sensibilities I unfortunately created such an immediate and profoundly adverse effect, by apparently mistakenly relating with naive enthusiasm details of my employment as a builder's labourer, that she had convinced herself of my ineligibility as escort to her daughter before we reached the jelly and custard.

"Mummy doesn't want me to go out with you anymore."

Such hard-heartedly devastating words, uttered with all the conscious cruelty of which adolescent femininity is capable, while later sitting on the front garden wall, words which left me, after ineffectual apologies for my inadequacy, bereft with humiliating rejection, though mercifully my resulting rather over-dramatised period of romantic mourning lasted only for as long as it evoked any sort of sympathetic response from those of my friends who were remotely interested, which rather predictably turned out to be very few, though even this disappointment was somewhat ironically compensated by my brother Dennis accidently sitting on and shattering a rather resented present of an intended example of the young ladies always pointedly assumed superior musical appreciation, a recording of Mario Lanza singing 'Be My Love', my own tastes after an adolescence spent listening to the American Forces Network with my three big brothers inclining more towards Hank Williams and Spike Jones and his City Slickers.

Three weeks later, I was despatched to Mansfield to find myself standing before an excessively enthusiastic recruiting officer, who informed me that it had somehow been decided that my immediate future lay within the ranks of the Royal Artillery, and spared no effort in impressing upon me the advantages available if I could be persuaded to become a regular soldier as opposed to a mere national serviceman, and I, with more than a passing interest in the higher rate of pay and the promise of a tempting period of deferment to the date of my reporting for basic training, in a moment of irresolution opted for the shortest possible period of regular engagement, that of three years with the colours, a compromise in which, at the time, to someone whose career horizon had so far reached no higher than a building site ladder, the extra year seemed of no particular significance, while the decision also entitled me to the intriguing prospect of the presentation of the Queen's shilling, a tradition which I had previously imagined only existed within the pages of books by Rudyard Kipling, and which in reality proved rather less than romantic when the officer simply handed over a grubby 'bob piece' from his pocket and not some gleaming, specially minted coin in a velvet-lined Royal Crested box, leaving me to return home later that morning elated at my adventurous impetuosity, but more than a little apprehensive as to the ultimate wisdom of my decision.

Reassuringly, my parents' enthusiastic endorsement soon helped to dispel any misgivings and I basked in the warm glow of their approval, even if some of my friends, most of whom were themselves miners and exempt from National Service, regarded my signing away the extra year of my life as tantamount to committing suicide and myself as being little more than daft as a brush, but being of a family insistently encouraged to accept the consequences of their own actions and more than capable of enough bloody-mindedness to confound most opposition, I managed to get through the period up to my reporting for duty with a mixture of youthful bravado and pretence, and one bitterly cold morning finally made my farewells to the family, or at least to my parents and Monty the dog, no other members being available, a slightly disappointing inevitability in a household where the amount of transitory migration always seemed to be directly influenced by the inadequacy of the available living space.

So, equipped with a tiny brown cardboard suitcase and a travel warrant to somewhere named Oswestry in Shropshire, I made the short bus journey to the town railway station, sitting on the front seat of the top deck and theatrically feigning my customary air of false nonchalance, which would have been rather more understandable had the bus contained more occupants than the driver and a conductress, who moaned about the inconvenience of climbing the stairway to issue my ticket and then spent the rest of the journey self-indulgently combing her long red hair downstairs.

Having alighted from the bus beside the entrance to the steep approach road to the station, I walked slowly up to the long grey-stone building displaying all the weary signs of neglect so painstakingly cultivated by British Railways and which hardly constituted an inspirational gateway to the beginning of my great adventure.

Then, having checked the details of my journey for the umpteenth time and exchanged the warrant for tickets at the tiny booking office window, I clambered into a third-class carriage to settle among the heavy acrid smell of smoke-soaked upholstery to be jolted uncomfortably from the shelter of the empty platform by a forlorn-looking engine wheezing with steam leaks and near exhaustion and out past the cattle pens, where in-transit bullocks occasionally took the opportunity of a water stop to escape and clatter past the high footbridge to indulge in a few moments of bewildered excitement, creating chaos among the shoppers in the town centre, pursued by panic-stricken porters.

On past the goods depot with its lines of wagons awaiting the arrival of the three-wheeled Scammel Scarab road units, which buzzed up and down the incline of the approach road making deliveries around the town; then forward to clank heavily onto the leaky old iron road bridge spanning the main road, which ran up past the sprawl of Messrs Oates' wood yard, a memorable wonder of tree trunks piled like twisted arms, its huge sawmill flooded with deep carpeted sawdust spilling out into the yard area, where endless lines of neatly trimmed timber were stacked like matchsticks to weather and mature prior to being shaped into hundreds of handles to grace the products of Stanley tools; the ugly elemental shape of the huge 'drug' road transporters roaring back from plundered local woods to be relieved of their loads by the great overhead crane to await the precise slice of the screaming saw blades; and the lingering pleasantly sweet smell of freshly cut timber and the ubiquitous dust that rose on the slightest breeze and blew across Gateford Road to sprinkle the walls of the facing Mafeking Terrace and waylaid passers-by with a fine white coating and stinging sore eyes.

On past the long straight parallel lines of the railway sidings, noisy with greasily unkempt engines pushing and pulling with awesome ferocity, wheels squealing and grinding, buffers clanging and crunching, forming and reforming dozens of trains to transport the coal, timber and produce up past the ramshackle cabins, where perpetually tea-drinking drivers and guards grumbled about unsuitable loads and missed opportunities for main line escape, and struggling shunters chased around the roadways coupling and un-coupling wagons with hook-ended poles, while across the mainline, where the Master Cutler blasted through each morning, the narrow Bonemill Lane sloped from the main road to mark the limit of the wood yard's spread, and at its lowest point junctioned beside an evil-smelling group of sheds, where lorry loads of animal carcasses were reduced to powdery fertiliser, and a cluster of small factories and foundries huddled in close proximity before a final boundary fence marked a stretch of rough open land, upon which sat the spectacle that was the Gateford Greyhound Stadium.

The racetrack on which hopeful owners, slippery bookmakers, minor league bad boys and gullible punters twice-weekly expected some skeletal hound to make their fortune was completely surrounded by a rickety enclosure hammered together by some enterprising and imaginative employees out of abandoned or appropriated gates, doors, bits of discarded railway hoardings, pre-war plywood boarding's, rusting chicken wire and an inevitable expanse of the ubiquitous corrugated iron sheet, the circumference of this sad-looking circuit being intermittently marked with spindly spotlights, which, when illuminated during the evening proceedings, cast a balefully harsh light that only served to accentuate the incongruity of the whole dingy arena, while the single stand, a high, wide and wholly unhandsome pigeon loft replica built from badly assembled blackboards, boasted an upper elevation, which housed behind its grubby small paned glass front befittingly basic bar facilities for the visiting VIP gamblers from Sheffield and beyond, and a public address system, which when operated sounded like Moses calling from the Mount, while below the narrow turn-styled stadium public entrance hopefully helped deter the underage locals, who congregated at most meetings to collect the discarded brightly coloured race cards, from sneaking in to badger some accommodating bookie into accepting pop-bottle-collection pocket money bets on some big brother's backyard-bred dog before being chased from the stadium by a cloth-capped white-coated steward.

Beside the stadium, a dusty track led up from the direction of the outlaying village of Shireoaks to pass the distant sprawl of black corrugated buildings surrounding the base of the high CWS Glassworks chimney, before finally junctioning with the main road where on one corner sat the Gateford Hotel, built in 1925 to accommodate the residents and workers of the ever-increasing straggle of homes and industry, following the route of the railway out towards the old established agricultural land and, in common with most buildings after a wartime without paint or maintenance, now looking desperately unkempt, its once impressively heavy cast-iron wall-top railings, balustrades and chains long gone in sacrifice to the war effort and reputedly condemned to rust away in some forgotten corner of Tommy Ward's Sheffield scrap-yard, when the wizards of Whitehall finally recognised that the 'most vital half mile in England' (W S Churchill's words) was more than capable of producing steel faster and more efficiently, and without the appropriation of decorative features manufactured from unsuitable raw materials, than they the civil servants could organise the production of munitions.

At the rear of the public house and facing the greyhound stadium lay the neat and compact, assiduously cut bowling green, where the area's flat-capped old boys sat in collarless shirts with sleeves rolled up in summer sunshine, devouring pipes full of foul-smelling Black Shag tobacco and speaking knowingly of pigeons, pigs and allotments, while scruffy kids fidgeted in the smoke-choking Jug and Bottle among the 'just a glass of stout' housewives, and stretched with hands hardly able to reach the tiny serving hatch to struggle with pop bottles filled with father's after-dinner tipple before sampling the contents on the way home, and concocting cock and bull tales about the bottle top coming loose and the beer leaking out, or the old fool serving always giving short measure.

Across the roadway and opposite, but in line with the public house, a short section of terraced and two blocks of semi-detached houses stretched along the main Gateford Road before ending abruptly at a large area of open ground.

No.299 of the terraced block had, prior to the outbreak of war, been the penultimate staging post in my family's grasshopper progress from South Wales, the other temporary accommodations being at South Street, Thurcroft and Vessey Road, Worksop, and as these moves, together with the final one to 48 Dawber Street, were all accomplished within the period from June 1938 to August 1939, the achievement must bear some small tribute to the determination and logistical ability of my parents in organising themselves, their belongings and eventually six offspring throughout it all.

The large area of open ground, which, pre-war, had been intended as a continuation of the allotments that lay behind a dividing fence just level with the boundary of the back gardens of the terraced homes, was faced from across the main road by the high-roofed squat shape of St John's Mission, the spiritual adjunct to the main Church of St John at the town end of Gateford Road, and was, in addition to providing Sunday School facilities, the educational starting point for many of the area's crop of wartime juniors, its plain brick façade betraying little indication of the interior's actual capacity, while its small front outside area was enclosed from the always remarkably traffic-free main road by a low brick wall and one of the few wrought-iron gates to escape the 'Beavers' over-enthusiastic great wartime metal collections.

Inside the Mission, an imposing set of polished wood partitions were folded back on large brass hinges each morning for assembly and prayers before being dragged together again to create the two classrooms where struggling teachers pursued the unrewarding daily task of attempting to provide some effective distraction to a world of bombs and mayhem for a bunch of working-class children with an attention span infinitely more influenced by where the Ack Ack guns and Barrage Balloons were positioned than tales of hobgoblins, gnomes and giants.

Of course, no one ever expected to discover any great intellectual potential, or could, if they had, offer much in the way of encouragement even into the halls of the senior schools, as the low expectations born of low opportunities produced little more than an occasional shopkeeper, clerk, a few apprentices and plenty of fodder for the factories, farms and mines, with enough left over to satisfy the local recruiting officers of the Sherwood Foresters.

Little significant change had occurred at that point since the First World War, and the situation was not about to offer any realistic hope until the end of the Second World War signalled the creation of a new climate of sociological expectations.

Any wonder the exploits of enumerable cinematically generated heroes, and even the less than inviolate real-life examples produced during the conflict, held far greater attraction and disproportionate influence over impressionable minds than persistent recitations of passages from Fred Kitchen books such as 'Brother to the Ox', daily wailings of 'All Things Bright and Beautiful' and most certainly repeated attempts to emphasise the significance of the times table to our future progression by rattling a wooden ruler over young knuckles.

We were, and would remain for far too long, remote from aspirations beyond the ineluctability of manual labour, and accepted our pre-designation with remarkably unquestioning compliance, created and upheld by both personal ignorance and enforced tradition, yet thankfully remained surprisingly resilient, singularly well-adjusted and implausibly happy, at least until adulthood eventually sowed the seeds of discomposure.

The world may well have been exploding into an inferno of murderous devastation and irreversible change, but at least there, in our self-effacing slice of the North Nottinghamshire coalfield, half hidden by the remains of Sherwood Forest and a Clumber Park littered with Nissen huts, new concrete and asphalt roadways, and packed to the pathways with munitions, we were spared the more dramatic effects of the earlier part of the conflict, which always seemed to involve everyone else in the most perilous situations while we suffered no greater engagement than the inconvenience of an increasing influx of military personnel to various newly established camps and installations, the gradual replacement of the Bevin Boys at the Gateford Road camp by Italian prisoners of war and, along with every other city, town and village, an all too evident adjustment to the populace as those eligible departed for military service and war work and for any number of other less than obvious reasons.

No.48 Dawber Street, which by this time had become the family home, and No.46 next door were the only two to be completed on a proposed new development of semi-detached houses originally intended to fill the gap between the top end of the existing street and the boundary of the lower-lying surrounding agricultural land, a development which was abandoned under the decrees of Whitehall with the declaration of war and left to provide among its concrete foundations and discarded heaps of soon-to-be grass-covered asphalt a reasonably challenging play area for we local juniors, and directly outside the front gates of the two houses on the uncompleted roadway, an extensive rain-fed sparrow bath and convenient source of mud for the under-eave nests of the annual influx of martins, swallows and swifts.

As to the house itself, it was, throughout our tenancy, a subject for much conjecture by the family as to whether the lamentable standards so obviously applied throughout its construction were the result of possible inordinate pressure applied to the builders to effect completion before hostilities began, or simply a true reflection of the landlord's incompetence; whichever was the case on first impression, and provided such impressions were gained from a reasonable distance, the block could appear quite a distinctive exception to the dull uniformity of the rest of the street, the windows, the doors and the two front corners being highlighted by crenulated brickwork patterns, which contrasted nicely with the sparkling crushed stone rendering applied to the greater area of the exterior walls, this initially pleasing effect soon becoming rather less than impressive with the early realisation that the stone coating had a persistent tendency to vacate the walls in alarmingly large patches at the slightest hint of any fluctuation in temperature, there to lie in great irritating heaps until Father, ever practical, swept them up to utilise as foundations for his decorative front garden edgings, while all attempts to gain entrance to the interior of the house by way of the front door were resisted so resolutely by the swollen union of door and frame that the family abandoned any further attempts for the duration of the war after the whole assembly threatened to collapse into the tiny hallway.

The interior of the house, despite the inclusion of one of the only bathrooms and inside toilets on the whole street, had actually been built to a design which had basically remained unchanged since the First World War, the tiny scullery being dominated in one corner by a large brick-built, coal-fired linen boiler, complete with cast-iron water holder and heavy round-board top cover, while the whole elemental contraption required a very large and heavy attendant mangle, a galvanised pot-bellied dolly tub, dolly-legs, a glass-faced rubbing board, several large blocks of sickly smelling Fairy soap, a good strong, sharp knife and a substantial hammer wielded by an arm powerful enough to chop the remarkably hard soap into the required size before any successful weekly wash could be contemplated.

Beyond the scullery was the front room – and that is precisely what it was, not a lounge or a parlour, but a plain, undersized and definitely overpopulated front room – which doubled both as a living and dining area, and contained the only effective source of heat in the entire house, the range, the only insignificant alternative being a tiny cast iron fronted fireplace which graced the main bedroom and was only ever subjected to an actual fire during 1948 on the occasion of Mother's recuperation from her hysterectomy operation, while the range, which covered the entire width and almost half the height of the chimney breast, could, when at full blast, almost shrivel the leg hairs of anyone lingering too close, even if its miniscule back boiler constantly struggled to provide a reluctant supply of tepid water to the big enamelled cast-iron bath, and the grate required a daily routine of maintenance of such bewildering complexity that my father deemed it beyond the capabilities of any other member of the family than himself, not that any other member ever attempted to dispute his assumption.

The routine, which always began with a laborious raking out of the previous day's ashes and invariably left the atmosphere in the room thick with acrid floating dust, then required a careful laying of several crumpled sheets of newspaper, specially cut kindling sticks and a few strategically positioned small pieces of coal before the creation received the lighted match and hopefully successfully ignited, then reached a sufficient level of combustion for a further crucial application of just the right amount of best nuggets, before being later topped off with a liberal covering of 'Slek', leaving Father to continue his daily homage to the great cast-iron construction by applying a thick coating of black leading to its entire surface and buffing to a rich, dark glow its complicated paraphernalia of oven doors, grates, damper handles, kettle holders and high mantle, then turning his attention to the ornate brass fender which surrounded the hearth and polishing it to a mirror-like finish before then, and only then, rousing his slumbering family.

That was Father; ever resolute in his absolute conviction that some things were, without prejudice or discrimination, his marital duty to complete.

It was to him as much a part of his responsibility to clean the house, help Mother with the weekly wash, cut our hair, mend our shoes, make our toys, and clip and powder whatever dog was at that point the family's resident pet as it was to grow all our vegetables and spend far too much of his undeservedly short span of life labouring to provide for his family with a pick and shovel deep in the bowels of the earth.

From just inside and to the right of the entrance to the front room from the scullery, but set slightly lower in the foundations for no apparent reason other than to facilitate one end of its length to be jammed under the overhead staircase, a narrow pantry or larder ran along the outside wall and stored within its cool interior everything from Cooperative Wholesale groceries, a wire mesh fronted meat safe, endless pots, pans and pancheons, and Mother's upturned meat skewer filing system, a lethal-looking improvisation which held impaled Divvy books, insurance policies, dog and wireless licences, old bills and an incomplete set of the family birth certificates, the one missing being my own, which disappeared during the great Eadie exodus from South Wales in 1937 when, or so it was whispered among my older brothers, the manner and timing of the move required the utmost speed and stealth, and allowed little consideration as to what might be left behind, while in that now unimaginable age when the importance of such documentation seemed minimal, the loss of my certificate remained unnoticed until 1951, when I left school and, upon obtaining a replacement, discovered my birthday had previously been celebrated on the wrong date, though this was also due in part to Mother's resolutely cavalier regard for all 'inconsequential' family details, her unerring response when faced with any request for pertinent details involving a particular member being, "Well, one of you did".

At the far end of the front room, at the side of the window, a second doorway led directly into the tiny hallway and it was from here that a short flight of stairs led up to the landing and the bedrooms, the largest of which overlooked the open space where the facing block of No's 47 and 49 would have arisen had Hitler's megalomania not intervened, and which, in addition to its main area, had by some puzzling architectural compromise also resulted in a small extension, which projected above the hallway and was just large enough to accommodate a single bed, yet so narrow that the only way to access the bed was by climbing over its end.

This structural oddity, in the never simple equation of accommodating eight bodies in less than adequate sleeping areas, was divided from the main area, in which slept my parents, by a casually hung blanket, and was throughout the war years nightly occupied by my older sister, Lucy Florence, and the final addition to the family, baby Lilian Maud, who had made her appearance in June 1939 at 299 Gateford Road, and to whom Lucy, whom my father would never allow to go out to work, in the family tradition was appointed nursemaid, a role which she conducted to such effect that more than one of the local gossips mistakenly presumed that she was the actual mother and memorably incurred my sister's considerable Celtic wrath.

Pride of place in my parents' bedroom was, unsurprisingly to us, reserved for Father's wooden toolbox, as large as any ship captain's sea chest and packed to the brim with what seemed to be every woodworking tool available to man, each of excellent quality, produced by Sheffield craftsmen with a degree of pride that was to become redundant all too soon, and the whole treasure trove stored in devoted protection three feet from Father's side of the marital bed, its contents ready to produce, when required, wonderful wooden engines, super scooters, sledges, kennels and huts for our ever-changing array of dogs and rabbits, ladders and a stylishly compact orange box-constructed home for my collection of incorrigibly house-top attracted homing pigeons.

Father's other talents, which were many, all eminently practical and each demonstrated for reasons of economic necessity or his instinctive compulsion to exemplify, if only to himself, an ability to rise above the intellectually undemanding brutality of the occupation circumstances had thrust upon him, included boot repairs and hairdressing, both executed to sufficiently expert standards to successfully deter the necessity of his family ever requiring the services of any professional, at least until the vagaries of fashion eventually outweighed functionalism.

His most surprising creation of all being the greenhouse, built in 1949 without the benefit of plans, if albeit with some contribution from two of his sons, Dennis and Bertie, who, being building site labourers, had enough expertise to construct the required low brick-wall base.

The greenhouse was of such dimensions that it looked upon completion as if it really ought to be located in some market garden and not simply in our back garden, its maximum possible glazed areas with each pane of glass diligently puttied into place along four-inch deep bars and with every item of bricks, wood, glass, huge tins of putty and even a 'Biltin Junior' coal-burning heater and heavy cast-iron water pipes to be fuelled by part of his

NCB coal allowance and a mandatory application of 'Slek', all purchased from Messrs Newtons of Worksop.

The motivation behind the construction of this quite remarkable greenhouse, at a time when most in his position were content with knocking together a few old window frames and flimsy boards in which to grow a few tomatoes, seemed to be his usual apparent compulsive need to prove, primarily to himself, that he was capable of achieving results beyond what his social status indicated, though being also aware of his only too occasionally demonstrated, slightly sardonic sense of humour, was probably also his way of raising two fingers to a world which had predetermined his horizons, and if, as a result, the most important consideration throughout his life, his family, benefited by virtue of an improved diet at a time when most working-class families daily consumed enough starch to stiffen a weekly wash, then so much the better.

Each season, every ounce of soil required for his religiously cultivated tomato-growing beds was laboriously shaken through a large wire mesh 'riddle' to a fine tilth, painstakingly steamed free of any undesirable invaders before being lovingly raked and planted with four rows of Ailsa Craig home-raised plants, two to each side of the greenhouse, there to be nursed at a strictly maintained sixty degrees of heat from the double tier of water-filled pipes running along the inside wall of the interior of the greenhouse, and later to be fed in devotion with the foul-smelling solution produced by suspending one of Mother's discarded nylon stockings filled with sheep droppings in an old dolly tub of strictly rainwater.

Above the centre walkway, his grapevine, which eventually stretched rampantly along the entire length of the greenhouse, in late summer sagged with large tempting bunches of succulent green fruit, and forever debased our appreciation of all other grapes. Cucumbers too, grown in their own later-added extension, rabbit-tail pollinated, as large as rolling pins and sweet with juice when stripped, sliced and presented on a bed of fresh lettuce with a cut of home-cured ham from one of the next-door neighbour's occasionally sacrificed pigs, and a two-inch thick 'doorstep' of Mother's home-baked bread fresh from the oven of the front room range, while the provider, absent as usual, would be making, mend-ing, creating or gardening, or deep in his mine with the unresolved hurt of his old family feud.

The second bedroom at 48 Dawber Street, which was slightly smaller than the main one and looked out from the rear of the house over the greenhouse and across the back gardens of Gateford Rise, the final street before the sheer drop into Messrs Turner's sand quarry, contained one double bed, in which slept Oliver Charles Thomas and Dennis Herbert.

Oliver, the eldest son, was film-star handsome with a head of dark, wavy hair, a room-illuminating smile and inheritor of enough of his father's obstinacy to refuse point blank to take part in any Home Guard activities throughout the war on the assertion that his nine hours each day down a coal mine was quite sufficient personal contribution to the war effort, and, despite the occasional intimidatory intended visit from the Military Police, had enough nerve and good luck to get away with it, while Dennis, in contrast, was always unobtrusively introverted and quietly dignified.

A small box-room wedged into the rear corner of the house completed the family sleeping accommodation and in there both myself and my fiercely auburn-haired next older brother, Bertie Alan, who grinned like a gargoyle, could talk the hind legs off a donkey and was always addressed by Mother as 'Baker' in recognition of his mirroring the looks and personality of her own brother, Bert Baker, shared space with a large glass display case, in which a thankfully stuffed, graphically posed golden eagle stood imperiously guarding the forlorn fallen body of a tiny blue tit and always appeared with yellow-ringed piercingly unnerving eyes, arrogantly dismissive of our uncontrollably chattering teeth and day-shirt clad bodies beneath the extra bed covering of Oliver's obstinately unused Home Guard greatcoat, when the icy wind blasted up from the low-lying farmlands and screamed like banshees across the wide-open space of the 'backfield' to buffet the bedroom wall during those much hated night-times of long war-year winters.

7. Road to Tinker's Green, 1954

The ugliest way to enter any city is by rail, and Sheffield certainly proved to be no exception with its clanking run past Darnall's industry-besieged station to wheel-squeal up towards the huge motive power depots, where row after row of reception roads were littered with locomotives dribbling steam and pouring smoke upwards to drift languidly then fade among the continual fuel of vaporous pollution rolling from the industry-encrusted hillsides and dark depressions of a city long resigned to its own hideosity.

A noisy grinding, jarring deceleration beyond Attercliffe to make the roll around No.4 East signal box and a final furtive slide to vibrate to an untidy halt beside the unimpressive functionalism of Victoria Station's platforms before clambering out among the self-absorbed activity and preoccupied figures, and escape immediately becomes a priority.

Thankfully, my deliverance was already waiting at Platform 5, and with an urgent restock of cigarettes at the kiosk and one completely ignored request as to the arrival of my train in Manchester to a porter engrossed in the pages of the *Daily Sketch*, I was soon being dragged over the Thos Ward advert-adorned grimy glumness of the Wicker Arches, accompanied by two giggly schoolgirls who contrived to conduct all personal conversation by whispering it in each other's ears, while being scowled at, quite ineffectually, by a large lady seated opposite bearing a remarkable resemblance to Margaret Rutherford and displaying the remains of some poor sacrificed fox around her undulating chins, while I demonstrated my recently acquired awareness of railway travel etiquette by assuming the classic pose of staring at the window to watch my own image reflected back against a background of soot and sulphur-rendered architecture, and settled to pass the time ruminating over my past eighteen years, an endeavour infinitely more notable in its singularity than for any part of its actual content.

Not that my youth had been particularly regrettable; unexciting yes, unremarkable certainly and hardly encouragingly productive in respect of academic achievement, but then neither academic achievement nor artistic accomplishment were considered of paramount importance or even expressly emphasised during my education, even by those unfortunate individuals struggling to administer a daily dose of elemental learning against a backdrop of social disruption and world uncertainty.

Lack of resources and a system still lingering in the 'instil a minimum, then get them to work' mind-set, and a traditional parental reluctance to contemplate much ambition beyond the earliest acquisition of the highest possible regular wage, usually effectively discouraged any pursuance of creativity, my own brief flirtation with the possibility of becoming an art student regretfully foundering before the greater consideration of family economics, despite having earlier survived the more physically emphasised setback of a swift slap round the back of my head directed by the personage of an overweight gentleman who combined the rather antithetical curricular responsibilities of Art and Sports master, and who took rather excessive exception to my rather good pencil reproduction of a book illustration on the grounds that "Copying is not art", a declaration which I, in my adolescent credulity, perceived as being a quite debatable premise, particularly if it is used as an initial aid, and is in retrospect really no more contentious than the once questionable use of photography in conjunction with painting; but as the admonishment originated from someone whose most evident association to his other subject was the fact that he was shaped rather like a rugby ball and conducted class crocodiles to the recreation ground, the only effect of his unnecessary reaction amounted to no more than a hardly surprising affirmation of my own instinctive convictions regarding education and a temporarily sore head for yet one more confused pupil.

Of course, as with most less than ideal situations, even our daily struggles to assimilate an education which was no more designed to accommodate the natural creativity of inquisitive children than it was capable of offering any realistic and worthwhile assistance to those with academic limitations, or the fact that the end results of any amount of effort by pupils would ultimately be prejudiced by judgement based as much on prevailing social standing as on sheer ability, nevertheless embodied certain undervalued compensations, for without doubt, we unashamedly luxuriated in our 'rapturous ignorance', even in the midst of all the muck, mayhem and militarism, and consequently enjoyed a far greater personal freedom and absence of pressure, at a time in history when it might be assumed that the opposite would apply.

The curving route out past the blackened brickwork and patched asbestos of the goods depot at Bridgehouses, followed by Neepsend's miserably self-conscious housing peering over soot-encrusted high walls at whatever happened to be thundering past, was as depressing a display of industry-imposed gloom as anyone could regret being plastered upon any landscape; grime-lathered blue-brick deep-sided cuttings lined the rail side before a backdrop of hazy faint fingers of innumerable chimneys poking like periscopes through an iron-grey smog, while the ever-present high-rising power station slagheaps, piled like improbable hillsides, stared back starkly naked, stubbornly resisting the disconsolate spread of scrub grass and dust-covered gorse that attempted to push upwards from the lower slopes, apathetically offering to moderate the effect of the monstrous accumulation of ash.

Meanwhile, we continued our journey, enclosed in the stuffy little cubicle, with the girls still wittering on secretively and the fox-fur lady, having eventually tired of her fruitless attempts to confer her personal misery upon us all, now gradually lulled into a state of semi-sleep, from which she occasionally jerked back into puzzled momentary consciousness with hard staring eyes, before finally succumbing to irresistible oblivion with her mouth open and top dentures drooping.

Wadsley Bridge came and went, one more sombre outpost of line-side factories and squat stone station buildings, and then, just beyond, the fringes of Beeley Wood gradually deepened to enclose our progress in the welcome relief of thick undergrowth and overhanging trees until we rolled through Oughty Bridge and emerged past Wharncliffe Wood to vibrate into the stark open spaces around Deepcar and Wortley, then began the gradual swing westwards to clatter through Thurgoland Tunnel and over Rumtickle

Viaduct up to Penistone and a resumption of the begrimed, dispirited ugliness of old industrialisation.

A final rattle past the eerie emptiness around Hazleford and Dunford, and we dived like a rollercoaster into the long black pipe of the Woodhead Tunnel to endure the stifling back draft of our own progress before dashing out again into the brightness on the west side, dragging billowing smoke from the Victorian portal and beginning the steady drift into the Longendale Valley to pass the winding reservoirs and drop towards Hyde, then nose our way torturously through the maze of lines serving Manchester's London Road Station, where I stepped nervously down into the bustling platform's clamouring echoes, deep, dark shadows and long, harsh beams of dust-laden light filtering from the huge arched glass-paned structure overhead, abandoned my fellow travellers with as little acknowledgement as we had mutually maintained throughout the journey, and, clutching my little brown suitcase as if it held the formula for the next big bomb, while at the same time holding on rather less effectively to a resolve not to succumb to my increasing sense of homesickness, headed straight for the platform Buffet.

The Buffet, which hardly justified an appellation so implying delicacy, and would have been hard pressed to validate the title of café, was all well-worn brown linoleum, low-wattage light bulbs, crockery-littered tables and nicotine-tinted décor, and offered the customary line in austerity catering of seriously stewed tea augmented by sugar, the texture of which owed a great deal to the number of wet spoons previously inserted, while one or two curly cornered sandwiches, with something self-consciously lurking between the slices, crouched on the counter top, thankfully secure beneath a dusty glass cover.

I settled for the less risky option of the tea, and having heaped in as much of the sugar as was possible without actually solidifying the mixture, then managed to minimise the excessive sweetness with a succession of Senior Service cigarettes and prepared to wait out the hour and a half to my next departure tucked away in a corner, reflecting upon the fact that I was now entirely alone in a city which, upon our approach, appeared even uglier and dirtier than Sheffield, and had the additional disadvantage of being further away from home.

Not that Worksop in comparison offered much distinction beyond its familiarity, with its increasing spread of council houses, straggles of terraces, cluttered cottages, a few undistinguished Georgian, over-elaborate Victorian and over-wrought Edwardian homes, shops, offices, public buildings and its forty-six public houses, fanning out from one colliery at the southern end of the shallow waterlogged Ryton valley and littering the parallel progress of the old Chesterfield canal, and the Manchester, Sheffield and Lincolnshire railway to a point just short of a second colliery at its northern end.

Even Dawber Street itself was no more than two lines of tightly packed semi-detached blocks erected in 1933 over the deep red sandbanks above the ancient hamlet of Gateford and its surrounding, soon to be increasingly threatened agriculture, with each of its painfully plain homes fronted by a small piece of garden, some actually cultivated and even in wartime bright with wallflowers from shed-hoarded brown paper packet stored seed and horse-drawn Co-op milk-float manure-fed roses, zealously guarded by sharp-eyed wives behind wavering net curtains when the local juveniles played rounder's, hide-and-seek or ralico, or had the effrontery to seat themselves on the low front wall.

Between each block of houses, a passageway, conveniently narrow and much favoured by those show-offs with a good head for heights, who would spread-eagle themselves between the opposite walls and manoeuvre upwards until their courage gave out, led to a shared backyard, with coalhouses, outside lavatories and enough yard space to enable budding impresarios and stage-struck daughters to throw a blanket over the clothesline as a stage curtain and offer the first public appearance of someone's self-conscious son juggling two old tennis balls, with a chorus line of "Challa Walla Woo Looing" playmates exhibiting a far less impressive sense of timing and rhythm as they waved their skinny little arms and wobbled to some scratchy Felix Mendelssohn's Hawaiian Serenaders record, dressed in old grown-up frocks and oversized high-heeled shoes, and with faces plastered with their mothers' make-up, than they demonstrated when rope skipping out on the street.

The back gardens, most of which stretched long and wide enough to enable their tenants to grow the basic essential vegetables, also afforded space for a comprehensive variety of what would today be regarded as a reasonable selection of stock for a rare breeds farm, with Rhode Island Red, Leghorn and Bantie chickens cattle market purchased as chicks and usually front-room range raised; ducks of all descriptions; homing, fantail, pouter and tumbler pigeons; sheds full of canaries and budgerigars; the odd tethered goat; boxes of ferrets for poaching; lop-eared rabbits, Belgian Hares and ordinary crossbred rabbits for pets or the cook-pot; plenty of Greyhounds, Whippets, Lurchers and other pedigree and mongrel dogs; a few slop-fed pigs; and, holed up in the landlord's bottom-of-the-street lean-to paint and equipment store, the doors of which remained resolutely locked between 1939 and 1945, enough half-wild cats to successfully deter any youngsters playing after-school street games from going anywhere near it.

There was, of course, also that scourge of the neighbourhood, the Jackdaw, removed from a local nest by some ecology-unconscious junior Tarzan, to be raised on bread and milk, the latter invariably from bottles filched from a neighbour's doorstep, then left to fend for itself during school attendance hours and, as a result, mischievously turning washdays into chaos by soiling anything placed on the clothesline and reducing any housewife who happened to venture into range of its malevolent gaze to screaming panic by its terrible war cry "Jaaark!" and vindictive delight in launching itself in a series of dive-bomber attacks, until beaten off with a clothes prop by some rudely awakened night-shift working gallant St George.

Washdays, of course, meant Mondays, the most detested day of the week. Mondays meant a dawn rising from the sanctuary of sleep, an early light-up of the big clothes boiler, then a day-long shift of continually stoking it up, an endless parade of big white sheets, steamily smelling of sickly Fairy soap and Oxydol, condensation-streaming walls, fogged-up windows, rooms hung with airing clothes and everywhere the heavy sour aroma of hot, damp woollens.

Washdays meant Mother sweating in her wraparound apron, long straggles of blonde hair hanging from her turban, continual pulling and folding, pressing and wringing piles of shirts, stockings, jerseys and frocks, and Father route-marching up and down the garden path, arms filled with washing and watching for rain, bulging clotheslines and collapsing props, arguments with neighbours about garden fires, everyone in a bad temper, late dinners of Sunday leftovers and most housewives at the 'end of their tether'.

During the long summer holidays, washdays also meant 'getting from underfoot' and gathering the gang to cross the 'backfield', climb the battered boundary fence, slither down the small slope to skirt one of the least productive cornfields in North Nottinghamshire – a fact which was almost as much the result of the locals' self-assumed 'right to roam' as it was due to the land's unsuitability for producing anything other than high-grade building sand – and take a slow, noisy walk on the old public bridleway collecting cow parsley pea-shooters and hawthorn-berry ammunition, before reaching the five-barred gate that marked the end of the Ladywalk field and the corner where, in 1948, some Biggles-type lost his bearings and managed to land his Auster in the corn stubble, to later take off, cheered by half the population of Gateford.

Then on to follow the edge of two more fields and a sharp right turn before reaching the main A57 road, and a furtive grope under the straw covering of the farmer's long 'pie' to pull out a nice-sized turnip to provide sustenance to take us up to the farms and orchards by the old Toll Bar and Shireoaks Wood.

The wood, an untidy stretch of stunted scrub oak and birch, half-uprooted firs and hazel clumps which bordered the red ash track leading to the colliery, provided a much-favoured backdrop to countless imaginative interpretations of the adventures of Saturday morning matinee heroes and an always appreciated ever-productive arsenal of bows and arrows, spears and our lethal throwing sticks with the steel nut-weighted points, was where my brother Bertie Alan once discovered a pair of handcuffs, discarded by an escaping detainee from Worksop Police Station, and ended his over-inquisitive experimentation with him being led home in triumph, to be released by the auxiliary policeman who lived next door.

Entrance to the wood was not always a simple affair and sometimes entailed an approach that would have gladdened the heart of an Apache in an attempt to avoid detection by a family of red-headed hooligans who occupied the wood-side bungalow, and took particular pleasure in terrorising anyone they regarded as interlopers by chasing them back to the end of the lane and then standing defiantly across its width like pint-sized Vikings.

This temporary setback usually required a change of strategy on our part, which involved a long detour to come in from the opposite direction past the permanently smouldering sulphur-stinking slagheap and up through the coal dust-covered colliery yard below the high overhead wagon wheel like winding gear, rickety tin shack fabrications, littered rusting equipment, eternally squeaking conveyors and occasional sightings of helmeted, black-faced canteen-bound miners, their raggedy trouser legs rucked up by rubber-belting kneepads and tattered vests streaked with sweat-clinging coal dust, then past the ever-pluthering chimney loftily depositing a fine grey ash over fields and roadways, canals and coppices, and the much-prized blackberries and hazelnuts awaiting our arrival within the wood's overgrown interior, while opposite the pit top, along a small road that ran out from town to pass the abandoned flooded limestone quarry where the big boys swam and swanked to the village girls of Rhodesia and Shireoaks, lay our special hideout, where an ancient millside water splash dropped to bubble and gush by a field of inquisitive cows and, hidden from view under overhanging willow branches, large slabs of limestone jutted from the bank and juvenile imaginations ran riot with watery images of improbable adventures, before bulgy-knitted bathing costumes were spread among buttercups, cowslips and cowpats, as bony bodies were dried on one grubby pit canteen towel and the clang of buffers echoed bell-like beyond the pit yard as the oily steam-shunting engine dragged wagons of coal out to the marshalling yard at Gateford.

"Ah, yu gooin tu Oswestry?" The totally unexpected approach instantly startled me out of my melancholic musing, and having unintentionally deposited my latest partially smoked cigarette into my teacup as a result, I looked up to be confronted by a short, stocky lad standing directly before me, his russet and freckles-complexioned expression clearly indicating he was hoping he had found a fellow traveller to share his own apprehension on the final miles to camp, for when I stutteringly admitted that I was, he instantly sat down and began to grumble about the iniquity of the army press-ganging him into something that he hadn't the slightest interest in.

Of course, his complaints were not unique; most candidates for National Service at that point were infinitely capable of furnishing credible objections to having their youth disrupted by the demands of maintaining our oversized armed forces, but most, being more philosophically inclined, accepted the inevitability of their fate and attempted to get through and over it with a minimum of mental and physical damage.

Several cigarettes later, having resigned myself to weathering his gamut of grumbles, I eventually learned he was from Handsworth, the Sheffield district nearest to Worksop and the only one with which I could claim any sort of familiarity, having many times after the war boarded the white corporation double-decker buses with my parents to make the wandering journey though the villages of South Yorkshire to finally chug up the long hill through Handsworth's dowdy housing and down to Pond Street Bus Station to replenish Father's fretwork hobby supplies of plywood, complicated blue-inked plans, bottles of glue and fine file-like saw blades at a dingy old shop on the Moor, before sightseeing the city centre, dodging trams, gawping at the bomb-damaged buildings and reflecting upon our own wartime good fortune in enduring little more than the inconvenience of crouching under the lumpy-legged front room table when the Luftwaffe droned over from the east coast to ignore Lily Maud's screams from behind the screen of her ugly big gas mask, Bertie Alan's defiant demonic grinning from the depths of a corner armchair and Mother's impressively comprehensive command of Welsh oaths.

Naturally, my newly acquired companion was only too aware of how lucky he was to have survived all the previous madness, and had consequently determined that there was no way he was about to put himself at risk in some tinpot foreign outpost with a native population who had decided to make life as difficult as possible for any reluctant representatives of the remnants of British Colonialism the moment they realised that we were just as incompetent as anyone else, but despite the persistent self-indulgent grumbles, we each now at least had the benefit of companionship on the journey up to Chester and the final drag out into the Shropshire countryside by a labouring tank engine, which successfully confined our appreciation of its rural charms to little more than occasionally glimpsed panic-stricken herds of cows galloping to the far end of a field, hell-bent on avoiding the great clouds of blackness issuing from our noisy progress, while we passed the remaining moments of our civilian independence attempting to convince each other of our utter disregard for the imminent approach of our induction into all things military by effecting a display of bravado that owed rather more to the influences of James Cagney and Humphrey Bogart than any genuinely felt disdain, before the sad charade disintegrated with the realisation that we were gradually coming to a stop beside a long wooden plank platform and a board bearing the legend *Tinkers Green Halt*.

Our departure from the suddenly attractive interior of our corridor-less carriage was accompanied by yet one more of those unpleasant sensations of apprehension that now seemed to be occurring all too frequently, even if on this occasion we drew some slight reassurance from the realisation that there was quite a small crowd of other recruits gathering on the platform ready for the walk to the camp entrance at the end of an open lane and which seemed to be awaiting our arrival with an appearance of unnerving tranquillity.

Park Hall Camp had originally opened for the reception and training of future Royal Artillery personnel on the 29th of June 1939, so God knows how many other poor unfortunates had passed through its main gate before we, its latest challenge, shuffled through in civilian disorder to gather like unsure sheep before the guardroom and waited, dusty and sweating, to experience the first effects of what was to be, in all probability, an identical reception to the one that had greeted that first batch nearly fifteen years before, though ours would now undoubtedly bear the dubious benefit of the intervening years of additional rehearsal.

Suddenly, the guardroom door banged open and, as if propelled by fury, out shot two screamingly demented sergeants who immediately circled our transfixed group like ferocious sheepdogs and conducted some sort of ear-bursting contest as to which of them could produce the higher rate of decibels, while continually exhibiting a bewilderingly comprehensive vocabulary of invective.

The effect as intended, was instantaneous, with bodies bumping, staggering and stumbling as we struggled to interpret the incomprehensible instructions and were orally and physically bullied into forming two untidy ranks, and then responded in voices filled with fear to a shrieked name check before being driven off in a shambling straggle towards a long line of black wooden buildings, helplessly resenting the embarrassingly short time it had taken to reduce us to this state of humiliated abjection, and entirely convinced that this was the worst day of our lives.

Next, we were crashed through the entrance of one of the buildings and down a short corridor into a barn-like interior, to be allowed just enough time to dump our accompanying luggage onto two lines of beds before being rushed outside once more to stagger away, futilely attempting to achieve some sort of ragged synchronisation of movement without kicking the legs off the man in front, and being ceaselessly berated by our accompanying tormenters.

Then we were chivvied into a large storeroom and piled high with sour-smelling clothing and equipment, all thrown at us by assistant storemen, and each item's flying arrival, for some bizarre reason, heralded by its identification being shouted out in reverse order: "Pants Cellular, Uniforms Battledress, Boots Black" etc. with everything having to be stuffed expeditiously into a large holdall shaped like a boxer's punchbag, which was then rendered almost impossible to carry by being topped off with enough sheets and blankets to cover two of the family beds at home, before we were chased back to the billet to receive the allocation of our own bed space and disgorge a great heap of battledress, berets, boots, gaiters, interminable items of webbing, socks, shirts, jerseys, belts, mess tins and cutlery, and the occasional item of which the identity would remain a mystery for the foreseeable future.

We were next regaled with high-speed instructions on how we must immediately divest ourselves of all traces of civilian identity and present ourselves outside within fifteen minutes, suitably attired in pants cellular, vest, wire wool like shirt, hairy socks, unbending boots, thick canvas gaiters and over-stiff denim trousers ready for our first encounter with army cuisine, which, even when judged against some of the less than appetising manifestations of culinary achievement thrown up by the Second World War and its resultant austerity, proved remarkable in the ability of the Park Hall catering staff to reduce what presumably had been reasonable ingredients to an eventual state of unrecognisable mush, and was only ever equalled in its lack of appeal during my ensuing service by the stone-hard boiled egg accompanied by a cold kipper offered on a troopship during a Bay of Biscay force four gale.

After the so-called first meal, which was of course accompanied by catcalls of "Get some service in!" and "You'll be sorry!" from onlooking bods who had recognisably only arrived in the camp a matter of hours before we had, the remainder of that memorable first day progressed at the same frenetic pace as previously, and we were unrelentingly badgered, buffeted and banged about, dashing from one location to another in two untidy lines of demoralised individuals, each trying to impress the resolutely unimpressed accompanying NCOs and providing ample opportunities for hilarity among any watching personnel as we toiled untidily back and forth from the stores for greatcoats, badges, shoulder flashes and white lanyards, then to the barbers for the final crushing blow to our self-esteem by way of a murderous short back and sides, which instantly seemed to leave us all looking ridiculously alike as we returned to our future home and were instructed in the correct method of making our beds 'military style', the required layout of bedding each morning, together with a detailed demonstration of where and how each item of the bewildering collection of kit should be stored together, what pieces must be displayed on top of the bed each morning and even the position each must be placed in.

Next came details on ablution requirements, a term which momentarily baffled all of us until we realised it was no more than an example of military gobbledegook which meant washing, showering and shaving – the last two being for some of us entirely new experiences – billet cleaning responsibilities, times to rise, dress, parade, exercise and eat, with each instruction aggressively punctuated with dire warnings as to the inadvisability of any possible deviation, until our heads spun with the sheer overload of information and until at long, long last, the NCOs withdrew and we were left to collapse onto our beds in weary relief to conduct a few preliminary cursing, grumbling contacts and ponder the futility of ever detecting any trace of obvious rationality in anything the army required us to do, before the majority of us transformed into slack-mouthed, loudly snoring unconsciousness, and insensitively abandoned two inconsolably homesick unfortunates to their pitiful whimpering's and one determinedly defiant Glaswegian emphatically relating his determination to escape and return north of the border to an encouragingly attentive Liverpudlian in the next bed.

I dreamed of Mother that first night, standing by the long-gone coal-fired clothes boiler, smart as any shop window mannequin, short and shapely with hair white as snow tucked under one of her numerous personally modified Co-op Millinery Department creations, ready to indulge her post-war passion for taking sweet tea and slab cake with her cronies at the Picture House café, her youngest daughter, Lily Maud, ready to accompany her, wearing one of the flowery-patterned frocks which always seemed to touch no part of her tiny body but her bony shoulders and wearing Father highly-polished ankle-strapped black shoes and listening with eyes wide to Mother's mandatory warning of "Don't you dare show me up!", while I turned the big wheel on the open-geared mangle to force water from a freshly-boiled sheet and them both return later to find me nursing an over-inquisitive finger minus the tip, which had been surgically removed between two cogs, and have Mother, with her customary equability, simply push the hanging finger-end back into place and wrap it in a strip of linen with the reassurance, "It will soon grow back..."

This of course was entirely typical of Mother, to whom, after years of raising her tribe through constant strikes, mindless mine-owner lockouts and ceaseless 'making do' in the Swansea Valley, very little beyond an actual fatality seemed to necessitate an over-emotional response.

To her, even the Second World War always appeared to be little more than an inconvenience, which she regarded herself as more than adequately experienced and equipped to deal with and in fact seemed to increase her resolute determination to pull us all through it by whatever means she deemed necessary, which included a characteristically nonchalant rejection of the 'Beware the Black Market' exhortations from well-fed government representatives and prying officialdom.

Her determinedly singular approach to it all may well have lacked Stafford Cripps' sense of high morality or qualified her as an ideal illustration of Winston Churchill's interpretation of patriotism, but then neither of those privileged gentlemen had a cat in hell's chance of ever convincing her she was pursuing anything remotely amoral and not simply demonstrating, in her opinion, a perfectly justifiable reaction to a society which had for far too long demonstrated its utter disdain as to how her family or she survived, while any mention of Churchill invariably induced a response that was diametrically opposed to the great man's personal opinion of his own worth anyway.

"War-mongering old bugger!" was the frequently and vociferously expressed assessment by both my parents, and one based upon a great deal of sacrifice and adverse experience in one of the most deprived areas, at a time when Churchill's appreciation of the qualities of those he had in the past, and would again call upon to help fulfil his destiny, was less than magnanimous, and established his reputation as an overly ambitious, self-serving, wilfully manipulative politician who was quite prepared to invoke inflammatory references to the working classes as the enemy, indulge in melodramatic rhetorical demands such as 'unconditional surrender' or provocatively parade armoured cars through the streets of London when confronted by an intensely patriotic section of the population attempting to achieve a long overdue measure of social justice, who had repeatedly demonstrated their absolute loyalty to monarch and country through all his and many other political and military leaders' corpse-littered and casualty-laden exploits and barmy excursions into the profligate waste of the one asset they all depended upon, yet invariably regarded with such easily compromised compassion.

The next morning, our first as genuine 'squaddies', began as each and every one would throughout the eight weeks of our basic training with a reluctant rising, noisily induced by our newly appointed sub-section NCO, Lance Bombardier Muzzle, an Audie Murphy-sized bundle of self-conscious insecurity, with a pout reminiscent of Brigitte Bardot, a touching propensity to blush and the personal charisma of Goofy, followed by 'ablutions', with compulsory shaving accomplished by some with more evidence of blood than hopefully all of us were ever likely to experience as defenders of the remnants of the British empire; dressing, making beds and painstakingly laying out kit with all the pedantic attention to detail demanded and enforced by NCOs no longer themselves subject to its exasperatingly absurd trivialities came next, and then parading outside to march to the canteen while calling out hopefully correct indications of which leg we were putting forward and sounding like some band of cretinous morons to queue for a large greasy breakfast doled out by apathetic members of the Women's Royal Army Corps.

After breakfast, the rest of each day would dissolve into more queues for sadistically administered blunt needle inoculations against whatever the army thought we might be in danger of succumbing to while enjoying their hospitality; long lectures on every subject from regimental traditions, rank recognition, personal hygiene and the dire consequences of contracting anything medically unpleasant while enjoying anyone else's hospitality; and our first shambolic introductions to the foot and small arms weapons drill, all of which required a combination of physical dexterity, coordination and an ability to simultaneously recite the first three figures of mathematics, which seemed alarmingly beyond our capability.

We were also initiated into daily doses of physical training, a supposedly scientifically constructed series of gymnasium exercises and outdoor endurance undertakings, which would have been rather less resented had they not also created too many opportunities for the 'odd' questionably motivated instructor to indulge his personal propensity for inflicting unnecessary degrees of pain upon his charges, but as we were very quickly recognising, that was the army, and it was of no more use questioning the methods used to achieve the goals than it would be questioning the goals themselves; this was how it had always been done, and as far as the military were concerned, it was the way it would always be done, and any misguided interference or attempted repudiation soon provoked an uncompromising response.

Grumbling, whingeing and moaning were eminently acceptable provided of course that they were conducted among those of equal rank; indeed, some individuals seemed spontaneously capable of executing their pursuance almost to the level of an art form, while most of us rapidly acquired an eagerness to indulge in monotonous profanity and a propensity to exhibit only the minimally appropriate level of intelligence required by whatever we were expected to accomplish.

By the end of the second week of our training we were beginning to look, if only superficially, quite military, and had managed to absorb enough elementary competence to enable us to move around the parade ground as a unit without reducing Bdr Muzzle to imminent apoplexy, and in loud boots, baggy denims, blancoed gaiters and belt, scratchy shirt and with berets just beginning to betray the indications of individualistic styling so abhorred and persistently corrected by our instructors, we were already assuming a slight swagger of confidence in our deportment, and occasionally dared to presume we may eventually achieve some sort of parity with the standards expected of us.

The difficulties encountered in trying to match these expectations were of course as much an integral part of the process as the result, though admittedly unrecognised and unappreciated at the time, when every day consisted of continual agonising effort on our part and what appeared to be persistently over-indulgent criticism on the part of anyone of senior rank, a situation as with so many involving the military that was all too often pursued to a point of farcical severity, resulting in an incredible amount of our time and effort being slavishly spent cleaning, polishing, arranging and presenting the most mundane items of our equipment for inspection, only to have some almost incomprehensible accented example of assumed superiority from the War Office Selection Board heralded into the billet as if the future of the entire army depended upon his narcissistic capriciousness, to then invariably react to all our considerable labours with a demonstration of petulant vandalism, which might have appeared slightly less objectionable had they been circumspect enough to disguise the fact that they actually enjoyed their excesses, or indeed had we suspected that they were in any way capable of attaining a comparable standard themselves.

It was, above all, this pseudo-psychological approach to our training that some of us found the most difficult to accept, infinitely more so than the out and out harshness encountered in the more physical aspects, where at least each sweat-soaked, limb-numbing, heart-thumping march, charge, parade, double time and fear-filled attempt to drag one more iota of effort from bodies already in overdrive depended entirely upon the uncomplicated immediacy of our own exertions and physical limits, and not upon the interminable contrary inclinations of questionably motivated others.

No wonder over the ensuing weeks the NAAFI Club and camp cinema assumed so important a role during our precious off-duty hours, as it was, for most, difficult enough being banged up continually with twenty-five other disparate personalities, even if you are hopefully in pursuance of being welded into one unified entity, and as we at that stage had not yet earned the right to venture beyond the camp boundaries, there had to be some sort of respite from spending our evenings piling more bull onto boots and Blanco onto belts, gaiters, straps, pouches, backpacks and bayonet holders, relentlessly removing the last tiny scratches from cap badges, buttons and belt buckles, continually ironing our now supposedly tailored but still uncomfortably bulky uniforms, or simply lounging, ceaselessly smoking, persistently swearing or implacably bemoaning our lot from the prone position, writing begging letters home and reading mail from girlfriends, usually duplicitously hiding the fact that most of them were snuggling up to someone else each evening; it was either scrape together what little remained from payday after purchasing the one hundred and one items we always seemed to need and hopefully indulging in a few warm, sour beers, or sitting through a movie we'd invariably already seen twelve months before we joined up.

By this stage of our indoctrination, the few rebels who at the outset had made great play upon declaring an avowed intention not to cooperate, or had even indulged in one or more of the standard protests such as Blancoing their greatcoat or taken the occasional vain opportunity to decamp towards the surrounding Welsh Marches, had been dissuaded from any further dissention by a combination of ridicule, peer pressure and downright fear for life and limb, or had been spirited away to reflect upon the error and futility of their conduct in some billet with bars.

Naturally, no one actually enjoyed being chased, chivvied and chastised, and most recognised and resented the sheer lunacy of a large part of what we were subjected to, but by a combination of previously unrealised personal fortitude, a little help from those around us and the belief that beyond it all things must surely become easier, we somehow persevered.

Meanwhile, we had the prospect of a temporary release back into 'civvy street' to look forward to, despite it amounting to no more than being allowed to catch the rackety bus that served as transport into Oswestry.

Even experiencing the ambivalent attitude demonstrated by the residents of most towns subjected to an association with the military, certainly towards anyone of junior rank who has the temerity to expect anything other than a grudging resentment, was at that stage of our desperation hardly likely to dissuade us from at least attempting to establish some sort of civilised contact with someone other than the local tarts.

Sadly, we were to be just as disappointed in our naive approaches to the citizens of that smug little Marcher town-ship as had probably the majority of other homesick, over-enthusiastic squaddies before us, beaten by the prejudices and pernicious distinctions perpetuated by our national predilection for meaningless social divisions.

Thankfully, of far greater import to everyone in the squad was the approaching much-anticipated opportunity of returning home for our first leave, and at last a chance to emerge in triumph, leaner, fitter and hopefully a little wiser, ready to accept the plaudits of admiring family and revel in the opportunity to relate all the excruciating details of our painful transition from the gauche aimlessness of post-school irresponsibility into that weird mixture of manipulated potential aggression and unquestioning, if resentful, acceptance of the authority so effectively produced by the military.

8. Home Truths, 1954

The journey home from camp after our euphoric release was as memorable for the persistent itchiness inflicted by irritatingly bristly battledress trousers as for any belated appreciation of the rural tranquillities of Shropshire, or even the fact that the Pennines were now penetrated at Woodhead by a brand new tunnel ready for the shiny modern electric engines.

Worksop, of course, remained reassuringly unvarying, with the usual rumble through its northern outer jumble of woods to roll past the lonely outpost of Shireoaks' east signal box and then rattle down the long slope and glimpse the two final streets of Gateford jutting like landlocked piers above curving fields of corn and wheat, before finally juddering to a stop beside the low canopied platforms dotted with waiting passengers and lugubrious porters.

Leaving the station by the small back gate, I took the dusty red ash track that led back towards Gateford and passed the rusting ramshackle tin-sheet enclosure that surrounded Mr Lee's bus depot, stopping momentarily to watch the pigeon fanciers on the short line of elevated lofts opposite, rattling seed tins and critically watching their birds dismissively circling the high spire of St John's Church, before I turned right at the red-brick Stanley Street junior school to eventually make my way across the 'Rec', with its hordes of over-excited noisy boys in baggy blue shorts chasing heavy leather case balls across its treacherously stone-littered surface, pursued by gasping crimson-faced teachers who would much prefer to be lying in the sun with a pipeful of Erinmore and a copy of the Green 'un and pushed my way through the persistently reiterated gap in the much resented new metal fence and climbed the steep little street to emerge before the Cooperative Wholesale Store, to which Mother had always insisted I "run all the way" carrying the awkward shopping basket for blue bags of sugar with the 12323 'Divi' number drummed into my brain, and then marched up the main road flanked by the dowdy presence of poky corner shops and tiny front-gardened tidy rows of dark entranced homes graced with the names 'Neuve Chapelle', 'Verdun', 'Marne', 'Ainse' and 'Somme'.

On past the old home at 299 and the little St John's Church Mission, its final squabble of untidy five year olds long dispersed, and now sadly having to justify its continued existence by accommodating a manufacturer of electrical switches, with its frontage still bearing the concrete plaque commemorating the laying of its foundation stone by Councillor C A Longbottom in 1923; a short distance on, opposite the end of the street that so offended the hitherto unsuspected sensibilities of the landlord by bearing his family name that he insisted upon renaming it, a stretch of the main road led to the corner of Dawber Street, its street-end shop at the rear of the sloping concreted area once frequented by neck-craning juvenile wartime fighter-plane dog-fight watchers and pop-bottle returners in search of pocket money, Woodbine and Turf cigarette pilferers, boisterous ralico-playing street gangs and flirting couples, and here I turned up the rising road, ruefully acknowledging the universal disregard for my triumphant return from neighbours, who had probably never been aware of my absence anyway, and having disappointingly failed to detect any indication of the ever-inquisitive Mrs Crisp's presence behind the curtain of No.42 managed to disturb half a dozen sparrows playing at the edge of the big pool, before clomping up the pathway and opening the backdoor of No.48 to find Mother up to her wrists in flour, rolling out dough in the revamped scullery, the original coalhouse now having been sacrificed in the interest of modernisation, and the ugly, dirty coal-fired corner boiler replaced by a bright green hand-operated washing machine, which appeared to be only marginally smaller than the original, busily preparing batches of the beautiful-tasting small, flat griddle-baked Welsh cakes we always referred to as 'Picau ar y Maen', and which so effectively always increased my barrack room popularity each time they arrived by post during those first weeks of basic training.

Mother, who always displayed a relationship of easy affability with her four sons rather than any overly demonstrative expressiveness, particularly now we had all passed that indefinable point where she instinctively regarded each as capable of accepting the consequences of responsibility, or as she defined it "Could make his own bed and lay on it", on seeing my entry beamed her greeting across the width of her rounded face, and in that always evident light, slightly sing-song Swansea Valley influenced voice said, "Alright, luv? Want a cup of tea?", then wiped her hands on her flower-patterned 'pinny' and filled the big black kettle and set it to boil on her tiny new gas cooker, before following me into the front room, bright with its shiny-tiled fireplace replacing the great cast-iron range and gleaming glass-fronted cabinet displaying the pieces of china, figurines and general knick-knacks accumulated throughout her marriage, complete with the three elegant glass swans serenely sailing across the top and moulded by some artistically frustrated night-shift operator bored with producing endless lines of milk bottles and jam jars at the CWS glassworks, and proudly brought home by brother Den from his first employment.

Father of course was at work, deep in his North Derbyshire mine on his permanent afternoon shift, the loose grey skin of his upper body bearing the livid blue coal dust stained scars of numerous roof falls and burials, and would doubtlessly still be dismissing the irrational references of 'foreigner' directed towards him by slyly resentful 'mates' with the customary reticence and implacable dignity that were to me among his most endearing qualities, and to those who could never hope to understand him probably his most frustrating.

By this time, the rest of the family, with the exception of myself and youngest sister, were all married.

Oliver Charles, now thirty-three and even more film-star handsome, had married the girl next door, fathered two daughters and still worked, now reluctantly, in one of the local mines, employment he had taken up with typical disregard for his father's wishes just before the outbreak of war, with the stated intention of avoiding military service, and would always be the one most unlikely to accept any snide remarks from his 'mates' regarding anything approaching his father's equanimity.

Lucy Florence, my eldest sister, after a wartime spent working at the big munitions factory at Ranskill, had married a serving Grenadier Guardsman in 1945 and was now a resident of Merstone on the Isle of Wight, struggling in a dilapidated thatched-roof rented cottage of a fruit farm with oil lamps, one cold water tap and an earth closet, and contending with a vituperous old witch of a mother-in-law who wore what seemed to be an almost twenty-four hour head turban wrapped above her sun-wrinkled sour face, which to my mind always made her look like Geronimo, and who perversely made no secret of her alarmingly prejudiced assumption that anyone having the misfortune to originate from any point north of the Solent must be at best completely incompetent or at worst totally uncivilised, an attitude which caused a great deal of unhappiness to my dear big sister, and one which both my younger sister Lily Maud and I had experience of when we were 'got from under feet' during Mother's 1948 hysterectomy recuperation and packed off to stay on the island with Lucy.

Of course, for two ruffians already accustomed to considerable rural space and freedom the island was paradise, with acres of open fields, ancient farms and enough apples, pears, greengages and plums to satisfy even our austerity-enhanced appetites, provided we avoided the perpetual interference of the persistently grumbling Granny Long, who seemed to take singular pleasure in relating to Lucy every instance, real or imagined, of complaint, criticism or annoyance that we seemed to provoke simply by our resented intrusion into her sour little matriarchal domain; not that her constant whingeing and back-biting really achieved anything like the effect the old tyrant so obviously intended, as Lucy was always our protector, even in the face of her husband's conciliatory attempts to mediate, while we, armed with a natural resilience and the advantage of an upbringing in which the avoidance of adults whenever possible always seemed an elemental requirement, simply removed ourselves as far and as often, and for as long as we could manage, from her irritating attentions.

Among my brothers, Dennis was always the most unobtrusive personality, at times stoically reserved to a point of puzzling incommunicado, but touchingly endowed with his father's undemonstrative dignity, undemanding unless it involved the laundering of his enumerable starched white shirts, but frequently displaying great generosity.

He was, with sister Lucy, always one who expressed a genuine concern for the welfare of his younger siblings, and was now married to Margaret, his absolute antithesis; Bertie or Burt, he much preferring the Hollywood version, was my senior by six years and was the one upon whom genetics had bestowed a balance predominantly in favour of Mother's side, he being one fiercely auburn-haired, resolutely insouciant, headstrong individual who when challenged was certainly capable of demonstrating a willingness to resort to physicality.

It was he who, in 1947, melodramatically declared his intention of joining the Labour government's ridiculously incompetent proposed groundnut growing scheme in Tanganyika, then rather less theatrically quietly abandoned the idea with his eventual appreciation that it would involve leaving the comfort of home for a very prolonged period, and who after completing his National Service in 1950, the greater part of which always seemed to be spent at home, committed the cardinal sin of mistakenly assuming that the established family conventions no longer applied to him, only to find his ill-considered rebellion foundered upon the imposition of a dose of Mother's unique corrective behaviour therapy, which, on the first occasion of him returning home from a night out in the early hours of the morning, amounted to a severely administered admonishment, and on the occasion of a repeat performance a complete lockout, the remaining hours, despite abject pleadings for mercy, having to be spent in the decidedly uncomfortable interior of the coalhouse sleeping on a bed of Whitwell Colliery 'nuggets', and consequently suffering the extreme embarrassment of having to conduct his following day's employment as a builder's labourer in his best suit, a short sharp shock which effectively produced an immediate reappraisal of his behaviour.

That first evening back in the cosy unpretentiousness of No.48 began with little significant difference to most preceding evenings since I'd scarpered through the dark cloakroom and unimpressive side doorway of St John's Boys' School triumphant with relief and confused expectation, away from its scarily idiosyncratic headmaster who wandered around softly singing "Nymphs and Shepherds come away", and effectively transfixed the unruly with one menacing glass eye, the result it was said of an accurately directed porcelain inkpot from a particularly recalcitrant past pupil and the direct cause of his fearsome penchant for exacting instant retribution by launching the heavy wooden-handled blackboard scrubbers at the inattentive, a drastically effective method of correction copied by more than one of our struggling tutors, which resulted on one occasion in the offending pupil being rendered unconscious; away at last from the once-weekly insistence on reiterating our manual heritage and most probable prospects with half-day visits to the infinitely superior facilities of the Priory mixed school to noisily hammer ashtrays in metalwork and pipe racks in woodwork, and the much more eagerly anticipated opportunities to indulge our appreciation of green-knickers wearing girls in netball games; away bearing my embryonic lifelong interest in art; away at last to hopefully avoid the embarrassing spectre of repeatedly being reminded of my inadequate mental mathematics; away with the specious endorsement of the one-day visiting 'Careers Officer', who imparted his indifference with urbane expediency on a bench among the sour-smelling coat-draped intimacy of the box-sized cloakroom and conducted most of his apathetic listeners towards unquestioning conformity.

Once the remains of tea were cleared away from the front room table, and with mother washing up while duetting with Joseph Locke's 'The Soldiers Farewell' echoing from the depths of Father's latest slavishly polished radiogram, a quick lukewarm strip wash in the gloomy strong soap smelling bathroom and I was upstairs to pull a crisp cream-coloured shirt from its Clarks of Retford cellophane covering, check my slacks were suitably pressed and shoes cleaned sufficiently to satisfy my ever-observant father, from whom we all inherited a predilection for neat appearance, and I was out and away to take the short walk to where the East Midlands 'A' bus parked at the street end between the cluttered corner shop and the always well-patronised fish and chip shop, the driver and conductress huddled on the rear gangway facing seat flirting before the run into town, where I eventually disembarked at the triangular paved area jutting from the conjoined ends of the two roads leading in from Gateford on one side and the outlaying village of Carlton on the other, which for some obscure reason was always referred to as the 'Square', to make my way through the groups of long-jacketed, tight-trousered, occasionally incongruously hair-permed 'Boppers' gathering to bus out to the Nottingham Palais to pose around the bandstand before the visiting orchestras of Ted Heath, Johnny Dankworth and Tito Burns; past the arm-in-arm couples milling around the underground toilets waiting to cross over the main road and join the Savoy Cinema queue already trailing away from the stepped entrance and winding dutifully around the black ash-covered piece of open ground opposite.

One hurried pint of Black and Tan in the wide bar of the King's Head, with no visible sign of anyone I was hoping to see, and I was away over the humped roadway spanning the mud-brown waters of the canal and down into town to call at the Marquis of Granby and Queen's Head, only to find myself irritatingly buttonholed by the ex-girlfriend who had on her mother's instruction so unceremoniously withdrawn her affections before I was called up.

"Hello, Tom, where have you been hiding?" she cooed, as if she hadn't seen my photograph and my mother's proud announcement of my enlistment in the local rag.

"Avoiding your bloody mother!" was the best I could mutter back in response to her annoying presumption that I would be in the slightest bit interested in speaking to her.

"Oh, don't be like that," she bleated, "she was only doing what she thought was right."

"Well, thanks for the character reference!" I answered, and having no intention of prolonging further an exchange which was already beginning to expose a few previously concealed sensibilities, and having brusquely refused her invitation to accompany her to the local milk bar, I turned abruptly and left her standing, to push my way bad-temperedly past a group of nervous, obviously underage boys giggling at their own audacity in actually entering a public house, and headed for the low long shape of the Billiard Hall, hoping against hope there would be someone in there from the old gang, but to no avail; it seemed as if everyone that I wanted to meet had mysteriously disappeared, and there, in the smoke-cloudy, shadowy dimness, surrounded by stooping strangers mesmerised by the brilliantly lit green baize and the hall's permanent contingent of skiving idlers and perpetual scroungers, to the accompaniment of the incessant click and clatter of coloured balls and wooden cues, the sad capriciousness of youthful friendship struck home and the realisation dawned on me that time had moved on.

No one was about to wait for my occasional reappearances; everyone was now into new relationships and, if lucky, up to their arm-in-arm in love, and knowing most of my pals' terpsichorean limitations, nervously shuffling on the highly-polished Palais dance floor or clinging to girlfriends like limpets beneath the deep cinema balconies, resenting the intrusion of the usherette's torch, while I, like some irrelevant obsolete khaki outcast, wandered around hopelessly attempting to re-establish what were now obviously defunct relationships and begrudgingly beginning to appreciate the abundance of companionship back at camp, until having finally and reprehensibly succumbed to a mood of feeble self-pity, I crept into the darkness of the Essoldo Cinema and wasted the rest of that evening scornfully watching John Wayne for the umpteenth time personally conduct the conquest of Iwo Jima with all the excessively emoted bravado of someone whose always bombastic patriotism had stopped short of actually participating in the real war, before strolling home with a paper full of well-vinegared Whitings 'one of each', diplomatically avoiding the argumentative rolling drunks and smirking at the feminine squeals of "Stop it!" emanating from darkened shop doorways.

The next morning, Saturday, I helped Father in the big greenhouse and wondered if he'd ever been aware of the times I'd sat there hidden from view, learning to smoke with old vine leaves rolled up in a strip of the *Daily Mirror* and quickly came to the conclusion that he had not, or no doubt the three-inch wide leather belt he wore in addition to his ever-present braces would have been unbuckled and slipped from its position six inches below his trouser top with the occasional fearsome flourish, been folded in two and then snapped sharply back to achieve the dramatic 'Crack!' that so effectively reminded each of his children, at some time or other, that they were perilously close to the point of no return.

This solemnly conducted display, which was invariably induced by an exasperated call from Mother of "Chas, tell him, or her", remained throughout his lifetime as near as he ever came to inflicting physical punishment upon any member of his family, but always remained remarkably effective, if for no other reason than the abiding suspicion that each time it was required to be demonstrated possibly shortened the odds on the real punishment being applied.

9. Summer and Suffering, 1954

That evening, having earlier quite shamelessly exacted some unforgivably vindictive revenge upon the female genre for the still rankling encounter with my ex-girlfriend by mercilessly irritating my younger sister, and being determined not to waste any more of my rapidly disappearing weekend, I amazed my parents by deciding not to go out and, having reassured them I had not suddenly lost the will to live, spent a few pleasant hours impressing them with the trials and tribulations of service life.

Then, the next day after dinner, I quite resignedly made the return journey to Oswestry, only to fall asleep in Whitchurch station waiting room, to arrive back in camp two hours late and find myself placed on my first 'fizzer', and be paraded the next morning before the studiously authoritarian adjutant with all the gravitas the military employs for such earth-shatteringly important occasions, and having been duly reprimanded, be sentenced to seven days confined to camp, which at Oswestry was practically a blessing, and be lectured on the necessity in future of allowing sufficient time when on leave for any such possible eventuality, a conclusion which, had I been blessed with the logic of his hindsight, would probably have made it pointless going home.

Still, it was good to be back and see all the familiar uneager faces, and listen to the grumbling, griping voices, most of which indicated that very few individuals had accomplished a much more exciting or satisfying leave than I had, while the number of mournful tales of ruptured romances and missing mates only served to reinforce the growing impression that we were all being manoeuvred by circumstance into an increasing alienation from all things civilian, and more and more into complete interdependence.

The next morning, after the usual clamorous Bdr Muzzle motivated, less than enthusiastic rising from our beds, and my appearance before the adjutant, the remainder of the day progressed with an even greater sense of urgency than had any before our weekend break, probably for no more plausible reason than some punitive desire on the part of our overseers to remove any possible irresolution after our exposure to the corrupting influences of home.

Everything exploded into double time, with everyone expected to achieve everything in half the usual time, with even the diminutive Bdr Muzzle, who always conveyed the impression of being fundamentally ill at ease with his authority, managing to puff himself up to a point where his natural diffidence almost disappeared, but which also unfortunately had the effect of projecting his voice up a further two octaves, making him sound like some dotty falsetto, until with relief all around, relative normality returned and we diligently applied ourselves to all the rifle firing, marching, foot and weapons drill and fatigue that would take us up to the completion of our basic training and that much-anticipated day when we completed the course and 'passed out' to learn which specific skills someone had miraculously judged we were capable of assimilating, apparently largely from the results of a set of aptitude tests conducted with a set of small wooden blocks and appropriately shaped holes.

'Passing Out' day, even during the hours prior to its actual arrival, generated a remarkable air of expectancy throughout the billet, which would have been far more appropriate to the second coming of Jesus Christ than some ritualistic military performance conducted by twenty-six young men filled with questionable motivation and little realistic appreciation of the potential personal dangers incumbent in their newly acquired abilities.

Everywhere, everything and everyone was either scrubbed, scraped, squeegeed, scalped or simply slapped with paint, invariably white, to a point of absurdity; then the results were criticised arbitrarily to a point of illogicality, before a sort of compromise was reached on our part by making the most infinitesimal adjustment to whatever was objected to, or in some instances by simply ignoring the criticism and re-presenting the offending article in its original state, and on their part by either assuming or pretending that their persistence had finally produced the best possible result.

The great day itself dawned with all the lack of promise of a picnic in a ploughed field, it having rained throughout the night with a monsoon-like severity, which had left the parade ground awash with deep pools and augured ill for the prospect of twenty-six plus pairs of ammunition boots stamping around its expanse, or the likelihood of our razor blade shaved uniform creases surviving beyond the first 'about turn', but as usual, the army had the answer and subsequently utilised its most freely available asset, and soon had enough recruits armed with every conceivable cleaning implement arrayed along one side of the parade ground perimeter ready to move forward in line abreast and leave the surface in acceptable condition, while we who were directly involved in the show, having ablutioned, breakfasted and donned our impeccably prepared uniforms with a degree of care and attention, both in detail and effect, that would have gladdened the heart of Hardy Amies, then spent the final hour up to our curtain call rooted to one particular spot in the billet, frozen in abject fear that any unnecessary movement may reduce the crispness of a constantly ironed trouser crease, or dislodge some portion of the spit-stiffened glass-like coating of Cherry Blossom polish so diligently applied during numerous boring hours to the venerated surfaces of our big boots, or ludicrously trying to prevent any limb, joint or other physical protuberance from coming into contact with the inside of the uniform, a performance which resulted in a variety of quite credible impersonations of Frankenstein's monster.

The parade itself, enacted before a bevy of imperious much-bemedalled brass hats, our own nervously perspiring officers and those members of family who managed to find Oswestry, progressed without any great calamity or too many awkward embarrassments as we marched, wheeled, right, left, about turned and halted with acceptable unity and timing, and no little sense of self-importance, until the repertoire was completed and we were dismissed, no doubt with great relief by the commanding officer, to join the visitors and spend the rest of the day conducting proudly appreciative mothers, a few weepy wives, nostalgic fathers and the occasional touchingly loyal girlfriend around the camp facilities, then later that evening accompanied a definitely unenthusiastic Bdr Muzzle into the depraved temptations of Oswestry's nightlife, and guzzled ourselves into a state of inebriated acknowledgement of his contribution to our magnificent achievement, assisted by the town's notorious version of Quentin Crisp wearing a startling dress decorated with immense sunflowers, fingers covered in homemade tin rings and his/her companion, a skinny, mincing, hardly-out-of-school Kenneth Williams clone.

Two days later I was posted and transported as a potential driver to Kinmel Park Camp near Rhyl for a further six weeks of basic training and driving instruction, relishing the prospect of perhaps eventually manoeuvring one of the huge Scammel gun transporters around some exotic foreign location, even if my occasional scepticism told me I was far more likely to end up jeep-ferrying some alcohol-befuddled clown around Salisbury Plain.

Of course, first I had to actually learn how to drive, and doing it the army way ensured it was never going to be entirely simple.

For a start, there was no question of what one assumed would be the natural progression of beginning the course mastering something nice and small; no, it was a case of straight into a three-tonne truck, and if you passed the test then you might end up driving the smaller stuff, and considering the initially baffling complications of double de-clutching and very alarming handbrake-assisted gear changes halfway down the hillsides and bends around St Asaph and Colwyn Bay, it amazed me that I at least completed the course to the satisfaction of my instructor, even if during one of my less than impressive outings I did manage to deposit part of the lorry's canvas back cover onto the side of a large stone wall near Bodelwyddan.

The actual driving test system was simplicity itself, with four nervously hopeful learners jammed into the cab accompanied by and under the scrutiny of one of the camp's civilian examiners, all of whom had a deserved reputation for being extremely pedantic and not well disposed towards any upstart requiring their approval, probably with justifiable cause; though everything seemed to be progressing rather well when it was my turn to crouch behind the big steering wheel, until it came to driving through the town of Rhyl itself, where I committed the cardinal sin of according the approaching heavy traffic rather too much preference over my own progress for the examiner's satisfaction and immediately failed the test, and with the military's strict insistence on one chance only, possibly fortuitously sabotaged a possible future career as an East

Midlands bus driver, to spend the next two weeks resentfully nursing my severely bruised ego in opportunity to increase our military prowess, but with the unit being most commonly referred to as 'Con Troop', the suspicion was that it was actually somewhere they dumped the failures until they decided their fate.

In my case it was back to Oswestry once more for a four-week-long gunnery course, still indignant and rather embarrassed, but eventually accepting that among the rank and file no one really gave a damn about failing any course; in fact, with most serving soldiers being National Servicemen, participation was generally regarded as little more than a convenient way of passing time before demob.

The road to Gobowen and beyond was littered with the pulped remains of rabbits, some squashed flat into unrecognisable obscene patches, some mutilated into grotesquely misshapen little heaps of blood-soaked fur and sinew, while everywhere the blinded, bloated, plague-riddled, tumour-covered half-dead survivors staggered, squatted, crouched or lay dotting the tarmac, awaiting deliverance beneath the wheels of our rumbling convoy.

It was, after the pretentious pomposity of our departure from Park Hall, an uncomfortably brutal reminder that the very organisation with which we now laboured the guns, ammunition limbers and accompanying paraphernalia towards the firing ranges at Trawsfynydd had itself little compunction in positively embracing the development of ever-increasingly potentially disastrous chemical weapons, and regarded the conducting of 'volunteer' tests on naively unquestioning poor sods like us, with anything from the effects of atomic fallout at Woomera to the infliction of more subtle viruses developed at Porton Down under the pretence of 'cold cures' as incumbent in the pursuit of their profession, and probably requiring no more moral justification than had the appalling decision to produce the havoc now so distressingly evident around us.

On the gunnery ranges of Trawsfynydd no rain simply falls; it collapses in great eye-closing sheets which drench the whole miserable sponge-surfaced surroundings until the earth chokes and regurgitates the excess to slide in endless torrents down every gully, crevice and slope, until it flushes into flood and depression or bubbles into the over-exerted streams to finally flop noisily into the big reservoir.

To be thrown onto this fog-sodden, feet and finger freezing heap of miserable shaggy-coated sheep-populated moorland after the relative creature comforts of Park Hall, or even previous outings to the infinitely more accessible gunnery ranges at Sennybridge, was in comparison almost like being exiled in Siberia.

Hour after hour, day after day, it bucketed gallons of demoralising downpour around us, at us and on us, saturating everything and everyone, obscuring anything remotely recognisable and blanketing our world with such a depressing sense of desolation that we actually began to suspect the army might eventually surrender. But no, out we went, day after day, squelchingly hauling and humping the 25-pounder artillery pieces ever deeper into the creepily veiled dark-grey surroundings to position them on some swamp-like patch of heath, then firing off a few smoky rounds of high explosive into the impenetrable fog, with melancholic booms and hopefully in the general direction of the coast at Tremadoc, continually stampeding our eternally nervous "baa-baaing" four-legged companions into swathes of panic-stricken flight, then 'limbering up' and struggling sloshily back down to the dismal little Nissen hut accommodation to peel off our wet denims and leaking boots, to stack them around an inadequate pot-bellied stove to dry steamily as we jumped, stamped and shook the cold from our shivering bodies, and moaned and cursed the injustice of it all, then cringed at the prospect of tomorrow's repeat performance from beneath the comforting tightly tucked blankets on our sagging beds.

Tomorrow came just as determinedly waterlogged and despondently demoralising as each of the previous miserable mornings, with us being bullied, foulmouthed and fractious out into the downpour in ridiculous poncho capes and hardly dried clobber to gobble down breakfast over sniffles and coughs, then grumble out again to start up the reluctant engines and line up the ugly old Second World War Fordson Quads before the gun park's protective sheds, fill up and haul out the ammunition limbers to couple onto the Quads, then bounce out the 25pdr field guns to their places at the rear of the limbers ready for the slow slippery progression out of camp and into the drizzly mist towards the distant firing points, while we huddled together on the cab-wide gun crew seat behind the driver, already shivering uncomfortably, and as usual smoking incessantly until the order came to "dismount" and we tumbled out once more into the bleakness and began the usual scampering about, accompanied by insults and coercion by the NCOs to uncouple the guns and manhandle them into the allotted firing position, drop the big wheel-like firing platform from its travelling position and raise the gun carriage to drag it back onto the platform.

Next, haul the ammunition limber into place and open the doors to pull out the trays of shells and cartridges to stack on a large canvas ready for use, while whoever was designated as gun-layer set the target coordinates relayed from the technical assistants on the dial-sight and the rest of the crew waited with gun breech open for the order to load, then quickly placed the projectile into the barrel, where it was rammed home with force and the brass cartridge was placed in after it and the breech raised and closed, and we all stood like dummies until the order to fire was given and the layer yanked the firing handle, with everyone hoping the bloody thing wouldn't misfire.

That was the routine, round after round, hour after hour, loading and firing, constantly making adjustments to elevation and alignment, everyone having his own place, his own duty, and as with all things military, even his own gun crew number, everyone knowing where he should be, when he should be there, what he should have with him and what he should be doing, even if it was standing about doing sod all! And God help anyone who upset the routine, as routine was sacrosanct and ensured continuity, routine meant assurance to those who had to do it because it was easy to remember and reassured those who had to ensure it was done that we should know what we were doing.

When we finally withdrew from Trawsfynydd and left it to its lugubrious sheep and ghostly figures of caped and hatted herders on horseback, it was still raining, as if it had lost the ability or will to ever stop and for all we cared it was probably still raining there when we arrived back in Oswestry, bedraggled and beginning to rust, to start the long process of drying, cleaning, scraping and polishing every piece of equipment back into a militarily acceptable state of readiness for whoever it was required for next, for at last the time had arrived for us to disperse to whichever regiments of artillery were most desperately in need of whatever it was we were supposed to be more than capable of and, however superficially and quite often most reluctantly, attempt to make some small contribution to redressing the continually increasing demand for military support to our beleaguered establishments around the world by at last being able to soldier in earnest, doing what we had been for so long and at times painfully trained to do.

10. Autumn and Away, 1954

It was into autumn and the beginning of the short, sharp evenings, when after a weekend at home I delivered myself, via the echoing impersonality of King's Cross Station and a slightly bewildering introduction to the complexities of the London Underground, to Woolwich Barracks to await a posting to foreign parts, hopefully after the self-imposed hindrance of my less than impressive attempt to become a driver, to somewhere that the sun shone brightly, all the girls smiled like Debra Paget and the natives retained some appreciation of the benevolent advantages of the Commonwealth, even if at that point in history the 'Great Family of Nations' seemed to be filing for divorce faster than Roger Bannister went down the Iffley Road on the 6th of May.

The barracks, once you had come to terms with the impressive scale of its frontage, had passed under the entrance's great Doric columns and through the huge wrought-iron gates, then hobbled over the infernal cobbled roadways, may well have had a history dating back to 1776, but had obviously not been modernised to any great extent since the Crimean War and eminently justified the usual description of 'outside pomp and inside squalor', for which reason alone, in memory they remained to me very much less impressive than the photographs, always of the façade, convey.

The actual accommodation and administrative offices, the latter poky little rooms which always seemed to be at the top of narrow stairways, consisted mainly of two-storey blocks flanking three sides of the elongated parade ground, the lower level of the blocks, which beneath the slender cast-iron support colonnades of the overhead veranda had doubtlessly originally provided stabling for the gun-team horses of numerous artillery regiments, but now offered open-fronted, long steel-troughed, cold-water-only ablution facilities for the modern Elizabethan army, while the upper level hid behind its white-painted walkway the boomingly noisy wooden-floored, cavernous, continually freezing cold billets, which almost screamed with the imagined echoes of past armies and were now proving much too large and expensive for the present debt-ridden government, with its insurmountable other priorities to contemplate wasting its continual borrowings on, providing inessential items such as heating for its army, who were anyway presumably adequately equipped with greatcoats, heavy uniforms, jerseys, cap-comforters, gloves and one ludicrously tiny upstairs lavatory cistern anti-freezing gas-jet, around which we were expected to cluster for drying our daily scrubbed white-shoulder lanyards.

At that point, Woolwich was really no more than one great transit camp, and in common with all such seething transit camps and with all other such establishments, crowded to its inadequate canteens and overflowing lavatories with drafts of outgoing squaddies awaiting boats out to the remains of the Empire, and recently disembarked groups and individuals from countless regiments involved in every post-war policing commitment, politically unjustifiable rebellion, tribal conflict, uprising, brushfire war, far-flung garrison and United Nations involvement, and in which every dominion, colony, protectorate and mandate that we as former rulers of one quarter of the world's population still had our sometimes reluctant to withdraw fingers in.

Time-served regulars back from Korea, looking incredibly mature and swearing about useless Yanks and that bastard Syngman Rhee, and extolling the pleasures of Japanese brothels, ex Hong Kong bods, bragging about Nathan Road, Tiger beer, Happy Valley Race Course, ten-dollar short times and Kowloon brothels, sun-scorched squaddies from the Canal Zone swaggering among us white faced, been nowhere, know nothing newcomers, bragging about seeing the Suez Canal, Port Said, and claiming they wouldn't enter an Egyptian brothel under threat of death.

Bombardiers from Gibraltar, Malta, Aden and Ceylon, sergeants from Cyprus, Singapore, Malaya and Kenya, with everyone who arrived having seemingly been to where almost everyone waiting to go out hoped to go, and I, growing bored with the eternal hanging about, chose to disregard the old sweats' incessant assertion to "never volunteer for anything" and took on the job of runner, and escaped guard and fatigue duties by rising early each morning to light the fires in the tiny administrative offices, and spent the days bumping around on a bicycle twice the size of my Rudge, which had been built to the usual army belief that the 'heavier something is the stronger it will prove', delivering bags of 'bumph' to wherever it was required, and being always too busy to join the day-long queues at the canteen, somehow managed to survive on a diet of sausage sandwiches until the weekend, when my position unfailingly helped me wangle a 48-hour leave pass out of one of the officers to travel home by bus on Friday evening and fill up with Mother's cooking, before returning late Sunday evening carrying a large tin of Picau ar y maen cakes.

That, for a couple of months, was my routine, hardly exhilarating, but at least helping to relieve the boredom, avoided unwanted duties and too much time in the deep-freeze barrack room.

It was after one of my hectic weekend dashes home that on the Monday morning I clomped up the bare wooden stairs into the adjutant's office with his customary cup of tea as he reddened his posterior before the nicely burning fire I'd made earlier, while having no doubt impressed him with my ability to produce the heat he was now enjoying with a couple of pages of daily orders from his 'in tray', a few sticks and a shovelful of rubbish army-issue coal.

He looked at me with a condescendingly unnerving smile and said, "Eadie, how would you like to make this runner's position permanent?" and immediately frightened the living daylights out of me! Good God! This was just what I *didn't* want! Condemned for the rest of my service to a career of crutch-busting bike riding on cobbled roads, wandering around this bloody miserable London outpost like some homeless postman and kow-towing to a bunch of patronising clowns who weren't even capable of making their own tea and fires.

"Thank you very much for considering me for the position, sir, but I've set my heart on an overseas posting," I replied.

The remarkable self-control evident in my response surprised even me, and could only have been a habitually instinctive reaction to one of the army's many and varied lessons to 'Never intimidate anyone with a rank senior to yours'.

It worked too, as he simply shrugged, sipped his tea and returned to his desk to plod through the continual paperwork, leaving me to salute with all the obsequious expertise of someone spared a fate worse than death, then clatter down the stairs and rattle off, deeply relieved, to my next port of call.

Three days later, the long-awaited details of my posting appeared on the billet notice board.

I was to be sent out to the Far East to join the 25th Field Regiment in Hong Kong, and the following weekend went home to begin fourteen days of embarkation leave, a few uncommitted dates with an ex-girlfriend, plenty of reassurance as to their unbounded admiration from my parents that I should be the first in the family to serve in the Far East, Dennis having previously served in Palestine with the RAF and who made me a present of his own stainless steel watch, which some light-fingered companion later stole on-board ship, a typically ambiguous warning from Mother to 'keep myself clean', a few tears from Lily Maud and a resolute absence of any discernable interest from Oliver and Bertie, and then it was back down to Woolwich for a final parade and inspection with each of us draftees bulled to the limit, shined, scoured and scalped, and all of us bearing the Woolwich trademark of a still damp shoulder lanyard as we posed for the camp photographer who clicked away, probably intent on capturing the ultra-smart, clean-cut self-assurance of the modern soldier, but in fact producing a rather appealing reflection of just how touchingly ingenuous as eighteen-year-olds we actually were.

Early next morning, we were off, sweating, swearing, shouting and crammed into a troop train's airless compartments, struggling with piles of kit, bemused and blaspheming everyone above our own rank, left to pass the time smoking, gambling and speculating, and as usual, completely in the dark as to our destination, sustained by great slab-sided fatty bacon-filled sandwiches washed down with stewed tea as we rumbled through the drab shambles of some London suburb and then picked up speed to thunder towards our embarkation port, the identity of which, for the first few moments of the journey, seemed to vary imaginatively among most of the ports along the southern coast, and was finally decided upon as definitely being Southampton, but turned out to be Liverpool, where we de-trained late in the evening, stiff, tired and squinting into the begrimed dreary wooden ugliness of an Albert Dock platform to be assembled in the barn-like customs shed and subjected to interminable body counts and name checks, while the Military Police, who had conspicuously manned each end of the platform upon our arrival, now searched the train for anyone who may be belatedly entertaining doubts as to the wisdom of accompanying us on our great sea voyage, while a ridiculously immature-looking officer, whose experience of sea travel was probably defined by attending the Cowes Regatta, pontificated ineffectually about how lucky we all were to be afforded this extraordinary opportunity in this new Elizabethan age to see the world and serve Her Majesty, before dismissing us to our accompanying NCOs to drag everything along the dockside and gain the first glimpse of our troopship, the SS Captain Hobson, and then lumber up the steep gangway, clinging like mad to the safety chains and wistfully relinquishing our last physical contact with England.

On deck, the inevitable chaos reigned with everyone with a stripe bustling around, while we went through the motions and watched and waited, filling with melancholy thoughts and memories of home until we were allowed to clatter into the bowels of the old steamship to occupy what would be our accommodation over the next six weeks and to make the surprising and agreeable discovery that we were not destined to endure the discomforts of communal troop decks, but had been blessed with travel on one of the few ships operating under the auspices of the Ministry of Transport that had the luxury of four-berth cabins, and it was just before midnight, after stowing away our kit and having each clambered onto one of the bunk beds to sit and discuss the day's events, that my three cabin mates and I heard a deep mournful blast from the ship's foghorn followed by a heavy rocking movement as we moved away from the dockside, and with everything beginning to vibrate under the engine's increasing thrusting effort to churn the vessel out to join the midnight tide, it suddenly seemed so important to crowd around the tiny porthole and take turns peering out like prisoners at the image of a member of the Transport Police illuminated under a dirty yellow overhead lamp against the deeply shadowed background of eerie old buildings.

Despite our increased sense of excitement we all slept soundly that first night at sea; snug in our little cabin we burrowed deep beneath the blankets to be pleasantly lulled by the constant soft rumble of distant engines bearing us out beyond the indistinct coast and into the cold, heavy winds of the Irish Sea to awake next morning to the harsh crackle of the ship's Tannoy and a disembodied voice instructing us to assemble on deck ready for physical training, and experience the distressing sensation of sudden disorientation before rushing to the deck rail and, watched with delight by the luckily unaffected few, throw up violently into the dark green waters below, wishing to God we'd never seen the army and its bloody unstable troopship.

Unsurprisingly, breakfast was not well attended that morning, but a couple of hours later the majority of us had recovered to the point where we could begin to appreciate, if somewhat nervously, the size and power of the expanse of water around us, and ponder the sobering realisation that we were now at the start of a journey that would take us ten thousand miles in six weeks and were totally dependent for our safe passage upon a thirty-four year old Clyde built for the pre-war Burma run, single screw, originally named Amarapoora, Second World War hospital ship, latterly employed on the Australian emigrant run with a top speed of thirteen knots, facts which we decided if dwelt upon too much would hardly benefit our peace of mind.

Far better to appreciate that there appeared to be so little contribution expected of us, the cabins being cleaned each day by members of the Lascar crew, while we, once all the instructions on safety etcetera had been digested, were free to spend most of our time on deck reading and talking, playing cards, games of tombola, and only occasionally being called upon to take part in lifeboat drills and fire piquet duty, or reluctantly conducted to the stomach churning, vertiginous stern of the ship to bang off a few rounds with 303 rifles at wildly bobbing coloured balloons released into the churning wake, and which, in less than complimentary acknowledgement of our marksmanship, invariably sailed away unscathed to disappear among the great heaving swell.

Having been effectively terrified by lurid tales of the colossal storms we could expect when negotiating the Bay of Biscay by a group of Royal Navy ratings who were on route to HMS Tamar, the shore base in Hong Kong, we were all relieved to enter the legendarily unpredictable area in what must have been one of its more benevolent moods and thankfully pass through with remarkably little discomfort, the big single funnel pouring out its ever-present column of black smoke into a pale cloudless sky above an almost unbroken sea surface that was no more threatening than the boating lake at Bridlington as we passed parallel with the unseen coast of Portugal, and then turned east to enter the Straits and eventually crowd the portside rails to gaze upon Gibraltar's lopsided rock rising imperially through the soft transparent haze of early morning, its half-hidden harbour dotted with naval vessels, while just beyond, the curving coastline of Spain shimmered and sparkled as sharp slivers of reflected light radiated from the Gulf of Cadiz and we sailed blithely on to encounter a Mediterranean Sea which confounded even our accompanying naval ratings by producing screaming winds, driving rain and bulging swells that rolled to rise and fall with alarming ferocity, convincing some of us that the ship was about to be turned over at any moment, before Neptune relented and serenity and stability thankfully returned, and we passed the low smudge of Malta on our tenth day at sea.

Now it was at last deemed possible to erect a large cinema screen on the forward bow section mast to allow us to pass the pleasant evenings sprawled across the deck fortified by pints of unfailingly warm heavily malt-tasting beer, and gaze up at a selection of prewar black and white movies or the infinitely more affecting display of diamond-bright heavenly constellations glittering against the ink-black night sky, not that by then any so mundane a consideration as to how we passed the time, or indeed how much of it had passed, occupied much of our thoughts, an occasional wager on the ship's daily mileage perhaps, but there really seemed little point in squandering what was after all as near to a world cruise that most of us could hope to experience in counting the hours, days or weeks towards its eventual conclusion and the unavoidable resumption of all the irritating discipline and routine incumbent in our usual day-to-day existence; far better to appreciate the unexpected advantages, enjoy the opportunities and like soldiers anywhere leave the responsibility for our future to those only too eager to direct it, and upon whom we were never in a position to exert any influence over anyway.

It was around midday on our fifteenth day when, having been met by the pilots' launch just outside, we eased into the harbour of Port Said and anchored among the oppressively gleaming aridity blanketing the bleached municipal buildings, mosques and dockyard encrusted spread of angular inlets and jetties to await the formation of the next southern-bound convoy through the canal.

All around us oil-heavy low-sided tankers, ancient cargo boats from who knows where and anonymous dark grey cruisers, destroyers and myriad indefinable vessels from countless navies swayed gently against their moorings, or carefully manoeuvred into position, nudging their bulk forward and just occasionally blowing long warning blasts as a shoal of native 'bumboats' wallowed out to crowd around the waterline of the Hobson and other potential targets and hurled their string lines up over the ship's rail accompanied by the incessant begging and cajoling that Egyptian traders could produce so effectively, while the occasional inveterate individual who somehow managed to gain access to the main deck was unceremoniously despatched over the side by the ever-vigilant, only too obliging NCOs, the victim virulently invoking Allah's revenge throughout his short, speedy descent, with white cotton galabiya fluttering around his body like some ineffectual parachute, before he entered the distinctly unhealthy waters of the bay with an emphatic 'pluish!' as one more potential enemy of the British Empire and to loud cheers from his appreciative audience.

This perhaps extreme response to what was probably no more than some perfectly innocent, if over-presumptive representative of the native population trying to earn his next plate of dates came as no surprise to anyone watching, the daily papers back home having for the past two years continuously related graphic details of the effrontery, insults and attacks inflicted upon our increasingly beleaguered presence in the Canal Zone by the determinably embarrassing double act of Nasser and Neguib, while our own approach to Suez had been notably punctuated with emphatic reminders of the fragile state of Anglo-Egyptian relations, and that any misguided attempts to fraternise with the despicable Egyptians would be regarded as tantamount to treason.

Vigilance was the password, while it would have been extremely difficult to identify any member of Her Majesty's armed forces who didn't traditionally assume all Egyptians were dishonest, devious or downright dissolute anyway, and thoroughly deserving of a good dunking!

We thankfully departed Port Said later that afternoon, unimpressed with its flat featureless architecture and its head-aching heat, and chugged into formation to enter the canal, leaving the statue of its illustrious founder, Ferdinand de Lesseps, thankfully unwittingly gazing into a future where his great creation was once more about to become embroiled in the complexities of international political ambitions, while we less zealous mortals relaxed in the shade of the lower deck walkways and simply appreciated the sheer magnitude of his achievement, as the single wide incongruous ribbon of shining water glittered out before us, breaking softly from the bow of the Hobson to vibrate rhythmically towards the light bright sandbanks rising gently away into the surrounding low dunes, where an occasional village spilled its dun-coloured buildings towards the water's edge and the inhabitants worked and waved greetings, and the local exhibitionist gave vent to his anti-British convictions by lifting his galabiya to display his genitals before lobbing the occasional bottle in our direction, to be met with an appropriately abusive response from the ship.

As to the effect of the canal itself, even to a group who now regarded themselves as reasonably experienced travellers and had already begun to outwardly adopt a degree of blasé acceptance towards each new discovery, the sheer unimaginable originality of wandering one hundred and twenty miles through the most inappropriate landscape conveyed by the unlikeliest transport and gaze across at the incongruous sight of the towering superstructures of the Port Said-bound convoy apparently rising from the desert sands as they awaited our stately passing from their anchorage in the long El Ballah bypass, left all who experienced it quite literally amazed.

Around eighteen hours after leaving Port Said, we emerged from the confines of the canal proper and entered the great lake of Timsah, its blistering arc of unrelenting light bouncing from the smooth, still waters as the dark, elegant sails and sleek lines of countless native feluccas blurred beneath the suffocating heat, while their crews struggled to make progress before the powerless breath of an offshore breeze, and we moved from our usual vantage points and thankfully retreated to the marginally cooler shade beneath the lifeboats and canopied walkways, there to sprawl listlessly, avoiding any unnecessary exertion, drinking copiously, smoking endlessly, too overheated to eat or even speak much until the early hours of evening brought the bronze and gold streaked deep-red skies and produced a temporary, more endurable change in the temperature as the steady old steamer made the slow drag across the wide expanse and negotiated the short stretch down to the Great Lakes and out into the blistering stillness of the Red Sea, to labour down the coasts of Arabia and Ethiopia towards Aden and the eventually less ferocious temperatures of the Indian Ocean.

On arrival at Aden, we were neither surprised nor unduly disappointed to find ourselves denied the chance of disembarking even for the most perfunctory visit to its admittedly extremely uninviting mixture of barren-looking, craggy low mountains behind a foreground of grimly dirty buildings, stark dockside cranes, derricks, sheds and a general air of flyblown seediness, which all reinforced the impression that the whole dump had been set up to serve as no more than a refuelling point for the continual flow of shipping heading east.

We docked just long enough to pick up mail and provisions along with our own fuel needs, and just close enough to appreciate the town's varied and pungent ability to bestow the worst possible impression upon the olfactory sense.

It was without doubt one of the few ports we all agreed that we never wanted to see again, and one more of the outposts of the empire where we, as its most visible and usually only too available representatives, would find ourselves about as welcome as Hitler at Dover, but being by then increasingly made aware of many of the disadvantages of our often unappreciated or downright resented presence, but for the present to some extent cushioned from reality by the insularity of our shipboard community, we chose, helped by a modicum of typical youthful indifference, to afford any such rejection very little serious consideration, as it was to us, as usual, simply someone else's problem.

So away we sailed again, off into many more impressive sunsets, increasingly unloved and unwanted intruders in a world bent on rapidly rejecting the system that despatched us, each nursing his own personal resentments and all too often reinforced traditional prejudices, and leaving all those unfortunate fellow squaddies stuck in the frightful Crater district patrolling its dangerous dirty alleyways to rue their own misfortune at being just more of Britain's young men in one more impossible position foisted upon them by the worried mandarins of Whitehall; on through the balmy light of the Indian Ocean and up to Ceylon and its capital Colombo, where thankfully, someone for once had demonstrated a more than usual degree of perception by realising that, in view of the strategic British naval base at Trincomalee, it was worthwhile pre-empting the possibility of the island following India's earlier bloody example of chaotic compromise, and diplomatically granted it independence in 1948, thereby consequently reducing the risk of any in-transit troops being mobbed and lynched before we left the dockside, and free to agonise over no more than the choice of whether to visit the famous Hindu tree temples or the infamous lady and the donkey.

We left the ship at midday, stepping gingerly down the gangway in civilian shoes and olive-green trousers and jackets, with berets under the hard dazzle of a sun that bathed the whole glaringly white town in an uncomfortable atmosphere of breathlessness, and left us sweat soaked and extremely envious of the shorts and vest garb of most of the male population.

It was good to be on terra firma though, away for an hour or two from the restrictions of constant shipboard existence and its unavoidably repetitive contact with familiar faces, good to just wander the quiet palm-lined streets beyond the main thoroughfare, or just sit in some tiny bar, deep shaded from the relentless outpouring of incessant heat drinking ice-cold beers, and feeling slightly light-headed, and almost hypnotised as the unhurried pace of the town's daily life drifted beyond the doorway.

At four o'clock we returned to the quayside having neglected our sincere intention of visiting the temples, successfully deterred the purveyors of pre-war pornographic photos and stoically repelled the insistence of the 'lady and the donkey touts', and pulled ourselves back onto the ship to strip and cool off in our customary shipboard uniform of PT shorts and plimsolls while the crew busied themselves in their usual unobtrusive manner and the steamer wallowed away from its mooring, then turned with propeller churning to gradually swing around the southern bulge of the headland and head steadily east towards the tiny Nicobar Islands above the northern tip of Sumatra, then dip south-east to face Penang off the north-west coast of Malaya and pass through the area of water in which lie the remains of the great Royal Navy battleship 'Prince of Wales' and the battle cruiser 'Repulse', sunk so unexpectedly by the Japanese thirteen years earlier, before we ploughed into the narrowing channel of the Strait of Malacca to gaze in wonder at the luxuriously vegetation-topped outcrops rising dramatically from the viridian green waters on the way down to Singapore, an experience which left me with the indelible impression that here at last was the real 'abroad', the tropics, not the inveterately anti-climactic, high-voltage heat-blinding disenchantment that was the Middle East; here with skies gleaming with an almost transparent cerulean blue, here where inviting waters lapped in mysterious inlets against long ribbons of palm-decorated almost-white sanded beaches bordering the dark lushness of monsoon-fed forests and where every blatantly brightly defined outline instantly evoked the Technicolor images of sarong-clad beauties that khaki-coloured imaginations were only too eager to conjure up.

Our arrival in Singapore was of course preceded by the always impressive demonstrations of unhurried efficiency performed by the Hobson's crew when conducting docking preparations, which always seemed in direct contrast to the frenetically noisy efforts of the military in getting a few dozen draftees to form up with full kit in readiness to disembark and disappear into camps and installations around the island, or chug by lorry or rail over the great causeway and up into the interior of Malaya, precisely as so many of their fathers had done not so many years before.

We, however, under the critical eye of the duty officer, descended into the awaiting clamorous activity of the dockside godowns and set off in a variety of extremely uncomfortable transports towards the bustling narrow streets, ever eager to be set free from continual games of 'Housey Housey', the daily insistence on physical training and terrifying film lectures on sexually transmitted diseases, and experience our introduction to the exotic Orient, although when bowling along teeming market stall lined streets in fragile-looking trishaws piloted by wizened, emaciated, ancient-looking Chinese gentlemen stoically ignoring the proximity of bull-nosed overloaded lorries aimed by continually horn-honking drivers, chaotic rather than exotic soon seemed a more apt description, and we were mightily relieved to abandon our transport as soon as possible to find our own way through the crowds and into the mixture of sedately Italianate and low colonial-styled main streets to join the throng of service personnel at the Union Jack Club, and sit in its airy restaurant to enjoy the still singular experience of steak and chips with real Daddies sauce and PG Tips tea followed by plenty of cold Tiger beers, as if the world belonged to us, before later stepping unsteadily out into the balmy brightness to gawp at the colonialists' citadel the Raffles Hotel, with its ornate frontage exuding exclusivity and big shiny cars depositing white-suited planters, businessmen and administrators accompanied by overdressed wives or tiny Chinese ladies elegantly cool in slender cheongsams.

We even managed to contrive a peek at the other Singaporean symbol of English pretention, the great impeccably maintained Pedang, big, green and now returned to its obvious projection of implied racial superiority after the Japanese army had the nerve to terminally decimate the Strait's settlements' pre-war Somerset Maugham ambience, while to us of far greater interest and enjoyment was our promenading through the non-European influenced streets of unrestricted higgledy-piggledy homes and businesses, with confusions of stalls stacked with Technicolor fruits and mysterious vegetables, and hung with livid-looking cooked chickens and relievedly unrecognisable pieces of animal carcass, while street vendors cooked up large pans of steaming sweet-smelling noodles and the air was filled with the aroma of strong sauces, and clouds of pungent smoke from thick-rolled cigarettes rose above groups of pavement-squatting customers scooping thin steaming soup and rice from small white china bowls with ceramic spoons, who occasionally glanced up to grin a wide brown-toothed greeting at this latest bunch of white-faced interlopers, and graceful samfu-suited, neatly coiffured dark-haired girls clip-clopped past, conducting sing-song conversations, or giggled self-consciously at our obvious curiosity and approval.

Much later, and having regrettably realised we had insufficient time left to indulge in the attractions of Esther Williams in 'Bathing Beauty' at the Capitol Cinema, we made our way back towards the huge dockyard fortified by numerous Tiger beer stop-offs and then staggered clumsily back on-board the *Hobson* and slumped happily onto the bunk beds, to wake hours later with raging headaches and Singapore no more than a rather vague recollection beyond our moonlit wake as we drove on, porpoise led, towards the coast of Indo-China on the final leg of our voyage, blissfully ignorant and youthfully indifferent to the misery already fomenting in that unfortunate country after the humiliation of French colonialism.

The author, age 10.

The author, age 18.

Dawber Street VE party, 1945.

SS *Captain Hobson*.

Hong Kong 1955.

Gun Club Barracks, Kowloon 1955.

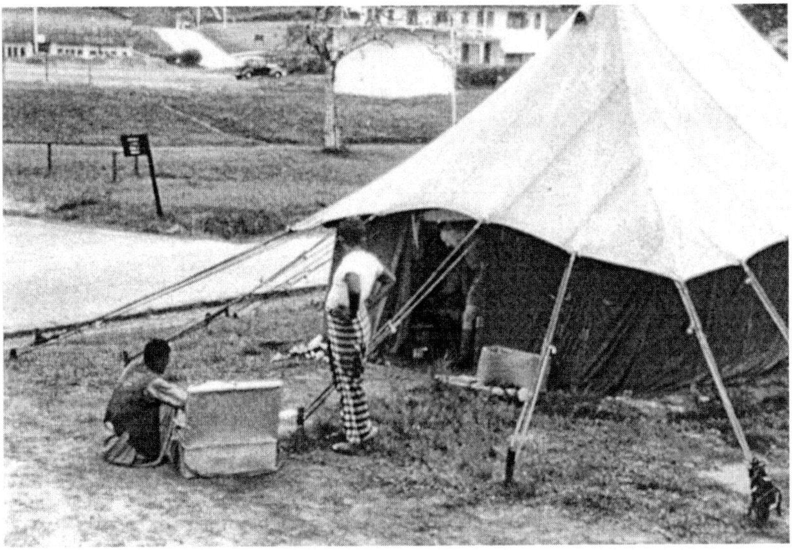

Under canvas, Singapore.

Food check, Sungei, 1955..

Able 4 at Sungei – author's impression.

Able 2 – premature.

Sungei Siput, author on right.

The road to the Cameron Highlands.

Boh girls, Sou Yeng, front left.

Taiping , Perak, Malaya.

Tent lines at Boh Estate.

The author, writing home.

Going home.

11. Hong Kong, 1955

It was Saturday and Christmas Eve 1954 when the weary SS *Captain Hobson* entered the narrow bay between the crowded shoreline of the Crown Colony island of Hong Kong and the facing peninsula profile of Kowloon City, crouching below its backdrop of white, villa-spotted low hills that hid the rest of the New Territories stretching towards the border with the Kwantung province of China.

Aboard ship, the excitement generated by the imminent conclusion of our voyage buzzed around the deck areas with an almost electric air of expectancy and elation, while our overseers, only too conscious that this was their final opportunity, proceeded to make our remaining time in their control as disagreeable as possible by pedantically reacting to each detail of preparation for disembarkation as if the entire future of the colony was dependent upon the potency of their irascibility, and not merely just one more bunch of first-time-away-from-homers leaving them to their fatuously tormented little world, though mercifully, even they failed to completely discourage our appreciation of exuberance surrounding the ship, as below and beyond its black and white lumbering bulk traditional junks with motor tyre draped sides criss-crossed our progress with seemingly complete disregard for any rules of seamanship or apparent consideration for personal safety, their pole, rope line, canvas awning and family washing cluttered decks heaving under blustery wind-bulged, ungainly-looking sails as they raced, lurching and rolling like flotsam across the bay towards the open sea.

Everyone was now intent upon crowding the ship's rails at every opportunity, eager to take in the first views and impressions of our future residence as we nosed through drab-green choppy waters beneath the soft luminescence of a December sun emerging through the last traces of morning mist over a harbour area littered with naval craft, lolling high-sided cargo carriers and low tankers, and teeming with fragile-looking houseboats clustering against the harbour walls in tightly-packed flotillas crawling with self-absorbed humanity, bony dogs and the paraphernalia of a permanently waterborne existence, or over-manned row-boats pushed from the shoreline to move erratically across the entrance, somehow avoiding tiny water-taxis jerking cross the surface, propelled by ragged little men wafting a long stern-mounted single oar, as countless daintily narrow-prowed boats manned by black samfu-costumed, indefinable-aged ladies in conical rattan hats scurried for safety, or wallowed about hesitantly as the *Hobson* finally, sluggishly eased and bumped gratefully into the welcoming shelter of Taikoo Docks, Kowloon side, to tie up alongside the feverish mayhem of dockside activities, accompanied by the incessant din of hooters, klaxons and the unmistakable high-pitched wail of Chinese voices.

We disembarked about an hour later, each of us banging down the gangway in now unfamiliar ammunition boots and bulky battledress uniforms, and hung like Christmas trees in cumbersome webbing packs, desperately dragging overstuffed kitbags and suitcases to be lined up and checked for the correct regimental posting and destination, then ushered onto the backs of a line of trucks and unceremoniously driven away from the dock area out into the thoroughfare of Canton Road, with every individual on each truck instinctively adopting that crucial precaution when being transported by any army driver, that of nervously white-knuckle gripping anything remotely rigid and hanging on for dear life, as we watched the long ribbon of family washing adorned, colourful banner plastered, white building lined road unfurl behind us, bustling with preoccupied inhabitants, before careering past the neat lines of cars parked beside the ornamental clock tower and dark spread of station buildings of the Kowloon–Canton railway at the southern tip of the city, to race up past the high blocks of the Peninsula Hotel on Salisbury Road and then swing left into Chatham Road, with all of us being bounced around among the piles of kit, until the clown driving, who was probably resenting the fact that our arrival was ruining his Christmas Eve, levelled out into the long, wide avenue of Chatham Road before finally swinging into a tree-shaded gateway to rumble up a slight incline and emerge once more into the light and the completely deserted, unmistakeably pristine rectangle of an army parade ground flanked by nicely proportioned, two-storied, flat-roofed arcaded blocks of accommodation buildings and the realisation that this at long last was Gun Club Hillside Barracks, home of our new unit, the 25th Field Regiment, Royal Artillery, the Garrison Regiment of Hong Kong.

Immediately after the lorry halted and the tailgate dropped, we all clambered down, hurling bags and kit before us, then crowded in the usual hesitant group instinctively awaiting the anticipated bellowed instructions and abuse, only to realise no one seemed in the least bit interested in our arrival, until a short, fat smiling Lance Bombardier emerged from one of the upper rooms and clattered down one of the two exterior conjoining staircases and halted on the wide, short central flight at the bottom, before eying us all quite benevolently and then calling out, "Right, lads, if you'll listen up we'll get you sorted.

I'll read out your names, the troop you'll be joining and where you need to go," and I, after hearing the inevitable Eddie, accompanied five other draftees to climb the right-hand staircase to enter one of the louvred double doors to crowd into a long, wide billet and experience the shock of seeing the central aisle littered almost ankle-deep in discarded newspapers, present wrappings, empty cigarette packets and beer bottles, while on the row of beds each side of the aisle various bodies reclined or sat slumped, almost completely oblivious and certainly disinterested in anyone or anything around them, and obviously painfully struggling to recover from the previous night's festivities, while we, the new arrivals, each commandeered a vacant bed space and dumped our kit, removed our packs, webbing, jackets and boots, and collapsed onto the welcome luxury of a conventional bed for the first time in six weeks, made a few hesitant approaches to the more sociably appearing of our new companions and eventually fell asleep, before struggling back to consciousness an hour later and wandering out onto the veranda for a couple of jokily posed photographs to mark our arrival and to gaze down at the large parade ground and white colonial-style arcaded blocks of accommodation and administration, and the transport and artillery park buildings spreading back among the tree-lined paths towards a line of low hills at the rear of the camp, where the wisps of smoke of countless cooking fires curled into the cool, bright sunshine of early afternoon from the shack- and hovel-strewn slopes populated by some of the thousands of refugees still pouring into the tiny area from the Communist mainland.

This then was our introduction to the Crown Colony of Hong Kong, thirteen years almost to the day after its surrender to the Japanese in 1941, that traumatic point in the colony's history which, in keeping with their emasculated over-sensitivity to anything likely to impinge upon their sacrosanct status, we were soon to learn appeared to have been conveniently expunged from memory by the colonial administrators and money makers, while we, their latest quota of apathetic protectors, determined to extract whatever enjoyment could be had from any opportune situation, while reconciling ourselves to the instantly evident, less than exotic reality of our presence actually being quite resented by happily exploiting the evermore indispensable dependence upon a few close confidants to help forestall any temptation to indulge in pointless introspection and melancholia during our confinement to the camp area for the two weeks of our 'acclimatisation', the worst parts of which, apart from having to rein in our youthful impatience and curiosity, entailed being bunged full of Paludrine anti-malarial tablets and enduring a vindictively painfully administered course of injections with arm-numbing after-effects against any disease thought likely to impede our fictitious ability to stem the Communist hordes at any time that Chairman Mao felt inclined to pre-empt the official 1997 return of the colony's control to China.

We also received ample disingenuous advice from the more established members of the troop as to the inadvisability of succumbing to the dubious Eastern allure of the overcoat-wearing and wax umbrella protected prostitutes who, each evening, tried to seduce the members of the guard while promenading along Jordan path, which ran alongside the camp perimeter wire.

Meanwhile, our first evening was spent within the prosaic familiarity of the dependable NAAFI, where we celebrated the safe completion of our trip out and our good fortune in arriving at the start of the festive season break, and commiserated with a couple of our number who had, on arrival, found themselves to be the recipients of 'Dear John' letters, with San Miguel and Tiger beer induced sincerity, and throughout the evening indulged in increasingly maudlin reminiscences with any member of the regiment who claimed to originate anywhere within a hundred miles of our hometown, most of whom were just too cash strapped to pursue the much more preferable delights of Kowloon City or Hong Kong side and were looking for a night's buckshee boozing at the expense of naive newcomers with plenty of voyage out accumulated dollars.

Later, when the NAAFI closed up shop, we all wobbled and collided our way back towards the high white barrack blocks, mumbling incoherently about eternal camaraderie between raucous off-key choruses of 'I Believe' and 'How Much is that Doggie in the Window', then dragged ourselves up the exterior staircase to blink into the brightly lit billet and slump onto our beds, uncaring and unaware of whether we were 10,000 miles from home or had just left the local.

Next morning, we were resentfully forced back into head-splitting consciousness above the still deepening rubbish covering the highly polished linoleum to experience one of those dubiously earnestly intentioned army customs whereby the officers of the regiment make the rounds of the other ranks' accommodation on Christmas morning to engage in a peculiarly British, slightly embarrassing to all, attempt to momentarily moderate the class barrier and hopefully bolster the esprit de corps by serving large mugs of rum-laced tea to we profoundly sceptical lower orders, who, had we the choice, would much rather have been left to indulge in avoiding all contact with anyone of senior rank, but which at least afforded us in the new draft the opportunity of a first glimpse at some of the individuals who were theoretically going to be in charge of our immediate destiny, and upon whom at some stage, God forbid, we may even find ourselves in the less than inviting position of having to rely on to ensure our safety.

We were already becoming acquainted with the junior NCOs, that is the bombardiers and lance bombardiers, they sharing our accommodation, while the sergeants, when they were not, as was the apparent custom with those of that rank, firmly ensconced within the sanctity of their own mess, indulging in gormless games that would usually embarrass the imagination of any juvenile, accumulating unmanageable bar bills and deluding themselves that it was actually they who ran the regiment, seemed to invariably be long service regulars with enough experience and savvy to determine their intention to get through this, their latest posting with a minimum of effort and inconvenience, plus the occasional newly promoted, misguided zealot who hadn't yet realised the fundamental truth of his actual ineffectiveness, all controlled and completely dominated by Acting Troop Sergeant Major 'Spike' Kelly, a six-foot-three, ginger-headed, freckle-faced, unpredictably tempered despot, who could and frequently did reiterate his authority by demonstrating his ability to reduce the most obnoxious little gunner to lip-quivering stupefaction by repeatedly thrashing the ground with his long, thick brass-handled and tipped-mahogany stick, while pointedly emphasising his superior height by fixing his squinting steel-blue eyes in a scarlet-faced glare directly above the miscreant's head, and then delivering a blisteringly vitriolic reprimand, culminating, if judged necessary, in a quite sincere offer to perhaps settle any further dispute more physically.

The Troop Commander, of course, was not among those who deigned to play Char Wallah to us that first Christmas, or indeed any subsequent one, the probability of which, we were soon to realise, was entirely beyond his comprehension, he proving entirely averse to or being incapable of pursuing any situation involving the possibility of approaching any affinity with anyone he regarded as beneath his WOSB-elevated eminence, which inevitably meant where necessary communicating by way of an intermediary, a personal foible which bore all the usual middle-class self-conscious determination to obscure his basic lack of confidence by presenting as few opportunities as possible for its demonstration, all of which, unsurprisingly, did little to enhance the opinions of those under his command as to his effectiveness or redress the very evident lack of respect forthcoming from his NCOs, and most visibly from ATSM Kelly.

The other troop officer at that point was a diminutive National Service 2nd Lieutenant, who during the months he was with us, whether by intent or otherwise, created so little impression that the most memorable detail about him remains the fact that he sported a cravat in RA colours, while his companion was a rather languid ex-Sandhurst 2nd Lieutenant with a large nose and huge feet, who always effortlessly imparted little indication of being particularly interested in anything much at all, but did demonstrate his technical ability during our time in Malaya, when he managed to achieve some sort of slight notoriety by being directly responsible for the removal of part of the roof of some poor unfortunate Malay's home with a misdirected highly explosive shell.

Naturally, it came as no surprise to soon realise that the consensus of opinion among the rank and file of the troop was that no one would voluntarily follow our leaders beyond any camp perimeter, and that the only individual who generated sufficient personal magnetism to warrant that unquestioning compulsion required to ensure motivation when faced with any kind of crisis was ATSM Kelly, though how much of his effectiveness as a leader was incumbent upon personal fear was open to question and mercifully never seriously tested.

Service in the Crown Colony certainly never produced much in the way of a need to determine who one would follow, it was simply a matter of doing as one was told while being agreeably cushioned from any obvious or imagined threat by the Colony's absolute and only too available hedonism, and accepting that even our secondary role of providing civil internal security was largely negated by the fact that the colony's police force was so numerous and ruthlessly efficient that we were very rarely required.

Of course, being the military, any window of opportunity was enthusiastically filled with any number of other areas of employment for available bodies, ceremonial guards, inspections of everything from vehicles, most of which were really only mechanically fit for being looked at, personal hygiene, accommodation, including married quarters, weapons and anything ranging from the BQM stores to the state of the perimeter fence.

With courses on everything from education – the military surprisingly showed far more concern for our basic academic achievements than anyone had during our actual civilian education – driving, though I'd long resigned myself, at least for the foreseeable future, as a failure in this accomplishment, and as much participation in inter-regimental sports activities as anyone with that sort of semi-masochistic ambition could hope for, and of course there was the everlasting over-indulgence in pomp and polished boots whenever any under-employed brass hat or politician at a loose end emerged from his ivory tower, or was despatched from Blighty to irritate Her Majesty's forces and inconvenience our for the greater part almost idyllic residence.

Not that we were entirely impervious to regimental pride or indeed individual conceit; we were more than capable of demonstrating enough of the showy military turnout to satisfy our betters, though given that we were, as was so recently illustrated by the Korean War, still equipped with tackle produced for the Second World War, all this pretentious parading probably perplexed more onlookers than it actually reassured, there not being the slightest evidence or suspicion that all our border posturing and dashing around the New Territories on mock crisis created any more of a reassuringly positive effect on the colony's population in 1955 than had those identically unconvincingly pretentious and unrealistic demonstrations prior to 1941.

Unsurprisingly, during our 'acclimatisation' period within the confines of the Gun Club, a great deal of our time was spent on the regimental gun park endlessly honing our loading and laying skills on the 25pdrs or sitting in the increasingly warm afternoon sunshine, lethargically polishing the dark-green paintwork and emery-cloth scrubbing the bare steel surfaces while gabbing about anything and nothing, and occasionally being directed in PT kit beyond the admin blocks to the slightly sloping sports field to enable some intensely determined sports-barmy NCO to try and ascertain whether any of us were capable of demonstrating enough athletic coordination and prowess, or were in possession of a sufficiently thick skull, to warrant consideration for future inclusion in the regimental athletics or boxing teams, but which, from our draft, produced no more than one over-ambitious potential pugilist, a misguided muscular Scouse who believed in his imbecility that he had identified an opportunity to enjoy some of the preferential treatment customarily doled out by the army to its sports representatives, but who prematurely ended his prospects by being rendered unconscious by a left hook from a thin-as-a-lath five-foot-two-inch tall Geordie in the first round of his introductory bout, while my own unenthusiastic displays on the field amounted to one feeble lumbering in the 100-yard sprint trials when I was comprehensively beaten by an overweight Cypriot, who looked as if he would be much better suited to Sumo wrestling, and two pathetic attempts to throw the old-type heavy wooden javelin, the first of which saw me fall flat on my face and the second achievement of hurling the missile a distinctly unimpressive eight feet to land just short of the instructor's plimsolls.

But as I, along with the overwhelming majority of my companions, retained sufficient male conceit and sardonic appreciation of military hypocrisy to in no way be prepared to voluntarily risk any painful modification to our facial appearance or any other part of our anatomy merely to satisfy the Commanding Officer's egotistical pursuit of reflected glory, my only other contribution to military sporting glory would remain confined to an ignominiously early substituted appearance as a goalkeeper during a football match against a victorious Malay village team.

On the morning of the 20th of January 1955, the morning after my boozy 19th birthday celebrations in the camp NAAFI, we newcomers, as a now integral part of 'Able Troop', left Gun Club Barracks for our first experience beyond its limits, and towed the guns and limbers down into the clamour of Chatham Road and crammed into the quads, wound our way with a convoy of jeeps, OA trucks and ugly little armoured cars, all proudly bearing the divisional sign of a yellow cockerel, out to the fringe of the city to cross Kai Tak Airport, with its insignificant control tower, aircraft hangers and Sunderland flying boats lying offshore in Hung Hom Bay, and laboured noisily up beyond a smattering of rhododendron- and bougainvillea-surrounded large villas into the New Territories for gunnery practice, thankfully with all the gun muzzles diplomatically averted from the frontier of the People's Republic.

The memory of our outing was ensured by it being our introduction to the suspiciously recognisable stomach-churning odours wafting towards us from distant Chinese small holdings and an eventual enlightenment regarding the true purpose of the large Ali

Baba-type stone jars dotted haphazardly around the landscape, beside which we excitedly posed for photos for home wearing our very new jungle-type hats and brandishing the old World War 2 Lee Enfield .303 rifles, and which in fact were the final resting places for the six-year buried then exhumed bones of some poor peasant's disintegrating ancestor, a discovery which left many of us sincerely hoping the environs of Kowloon City itself, which we had been informed we were from here onwards at liberty to enjoy, would present a more fragrant and less spooky experience, even if our very limited experience of Asian customs, personal habits and hygiene hardly filled us with any overwhelming sense of reassurance.

The day's exercise went well enough, it requiring little more than the usual begrudging acceptance of gratuitous personal insults while mechanically executing the same old movements and abilities with our accustomed lack of initiative.

We rushed around a lot as usual, dragging everything into position, and in response to the urgently shouted orders successfully despatched a few shells up and over the dry scrubby landscape to plop somewhere safely, hopefully without evoking too much protest from the ever-observant, hypersensitive Communist 'watchers' in the colony, took a break for a few sandwiches and tea, fired off a few more rounds, then packed up and thundered back to camp to find some idiot had left his rifle back on the ranges, and later that evening prepared for the far more important and attractive prospect of familiarising ourselves with some of the attractions we had already spent many an hour of our period of confinement being enthusiastically told about by everyone, and from some who's appreciation of the colony would never rise beyond the persistent opportunities to indulge in high-speed carnal favours offered by the dozens of no-nonsense young street girls from the entrances of unused private garages among the backstreets between the camp and Nathan Road, or the supposedly more permanent arrangements possible with the more ambitious downtown bar girls, all of whom seemed to be under the impression that their allure and sophistication would be in some way enhanced by wearing Westernised clothes as opposed to the far more suitable and appealing classic cheongsams and samfu suits, and adopting some ridiculous name such as Roxie or Alice.

Of course, at the other end of the scale there was also one determinedly sexually abstinent ex-grammar school boy who seemed to have embarked upon his own inauspicious moral crusade to convince anyone prepared to listen to him of the unique intellectual opportunity now open to us to appreciate the idiosyncratic mysteries of Confucian ethics.

I left camp later that evening attired in the almost regulatory-required short-sleeved open-necked white shirt, baggy-legged narrow-bottomed slacks and crepe-soled shoes purchased in anticipation from the regimental Chinese tailor and chaperoned by my newly acquired best mate, L/Bdr Harold 'Haji' Abrahams, whose nickname derived from a now largely forgotten Nat King Cole recording of 'Haji Baba' and who as a just-under-six-foot-tall, thin-as-a-taper, resolutely jocular, ginger-headed Scotsman was just about as far from any credible identification with the original as one could perceive, while I could barely conceal my excitement at finally walking past the unfortunate soul sweatily stuck on sentry duty at the main gate to step out into the wide boulevard of Chatham Road, then turn into Austin Road and through the madhouse of cars, lorries, rickshaws, trishaws, bicycles and ceaseless shuffling melee of always agitated-sounding pedestrians to dodge the sleeve-pulling ambushes and calls of "Here, Johnny!" from the persistent garage girls, then across towards the incongruously wide, untidily building packed and stacked, Chinese script-decorated, strip-banner-and-hoarding-hung tree-lined avenue of Nathan Road, which ran almost smack into the centre of the city from the peninsula tip to speed off almost vertically northwards, and there promenade with countless appreciative stops before the garish displays and be almost dragged into the brightly lit interiors of shops filled with extravagantly dragon-decorated pottery and the stuffy poky premises of tailors packed to the ceilings with roll upon roll of cheap cloth and untidy racks of ready-made clothing, with the back rooms rattling with the sound of flying sewing machines churning out two-day manufactured suits, all facing across the roadway the long tree-surrounded sprawl of Whitfield Barracks, with its dark lines of wooden billets from which bods like us daily vacated the spartan interiors to make the most of another cool, dry evening, jostling among the noisy groups and individuals of glamorously white-uniformed brash American sailors from the seemingly continually present US fleet, bronzed, always argumentative Australians, US navy hating Canadians, diminutive always-smiling Gurkhas and servicemen from countless other nations, all boisterously preoccupied with their own quest for enjoyment against a perpetually animated, continually changing backdrop of hooting taxis, screeching rumbling trams and eternally honking double-decker buses; the high wailing, whining cacophony of Chinese flute and dulcimer music; harsh undulant Cantonese, Hakka and Tanka voices; clanging and banging echoes from the KCR rail terminus platforms; the startling din of police car bells with black-uniformed officers intent upon harassing the backstreet gambling dens and dope houses; the deep, sadly sombre bellowing of departing ships in the harbour and low chug of the green and white Star ferries doggedly criss-crossing the crowded bay carrying silently dignified ancients in stark black attire; innumerable family groups surrounded by boxes and crates of green vegetables, agitated chickens and an occasional imprisoned pig, and all appearing to someone conditioned to the comparable moribundity of English street life intimidatingly unnerving but enormously invigorating.

Thankfully, at that time the main commercial areas of both Kowloon and Victoria had not yet been decimated by the eventual plague of ever-increasingly heaven-bound towering blocks of architectural eccentricities which have now effectively obliterated the colony's original singular identity of much more proportionately pleasing neo-Italianate, Victorian, Edwardian and colonial-style civic representations and shambolic appearing banner-festooned open-fronted, traditional-styled developments, which, for all their shortcomings, and recognising the inevitability of change, particularly by the Chinese who seem to be culturally incapable of appreciating the aesthetic value of any building over ten years old, at least helped retain some of the colony's unique architectural significance and identity, which has been so determinedly abandoned among the headlong rush to achieve 'impact' by excess, but to those fortunate enough to experience its previous infinitely less complex and intimidating personality definitely helped to produce and ensure the most memorably evocative of experiences.

By February 1955 we of the new draft were all accepted as a necessary part of the regiment, well able to stand alongside the more senior members on guard duties, weapon-firing exercises, irksome parades and holding our own among the mad, mad whirl of temptations, inducements and offerings open to anyone in the colony with a dollar in his pocket, and were just as inclined to avoid most responsibility and quite indifferently prepared to rely upon any individual who regarded himself as more accomplished or, as was usually the case, could be conned into believing himself so, particularly during the many occasions we found ourselves sweatily trudging about, disorientated or downright lost in the high rolling hills around the New Territories' reservoirs on map-reading exercises, to more than once venture upon some still recognisable Second World War defensive position, its fire-scorched area and bullet-chipped black rock outcrops chiselled with regimental insignias and scrawled poignant last messages from its beleaguered despairing occupants.

Occasionally, of course, we would be escorted, bulled to the eyebrows, to Star ferry ride over the bay to Hong Kong side to mount guard on the Governor's official residence, sitting befittingly impressively beside the splendour of Statue Square in Victoria before its backdrop of steep deep-green hills, and where it was not unknown for an unfortunate representative of the numerous young female bearers of cinema usherette style trays of Marvel cigarettes and Penguin chocolate biscuits, when not being duped by obvious nom de plumes such as Robin Hood, Sherlock Holmes or Dick Barton being earnestly scribbled on their credit pad, were enticed, solicitously helped over the wire, relieved of their wares and tossed back in the street, in one of the more regrettable examples of over-enthusiastic bullying so liable wherever young men are accommodated, and contributed so negatively and, unfortunately, so disproportionately to the military's reputation.

What was always a vehemently resented and appeared to be a grossly unfair proportion of everyone's evenings was spent parading in pairs along the well-worn pathways around the inside of the perimeter wire of Gun Club Barracks itself, less than reassuringly armed with pickaxe handles and presumably as the camp's first line of defence against any suddenly materialising Communist horde or more likely civil disobedient shack squatters, a duty which at some point in its largely boringly uneventful execution involved mercilessly irritating the corresponding patrol of town 'Taggies' with remarkably complicated proposals to achieve sexual union from opposite sides of the hardly conducive small mesh wire division, and which when rumbled, usually as a result of someone being incapable of sustaining the pretence and bursting into laughter, inevitably resulted in the understandably less than appreciative girls spitting streams of incomprehensible invective in our direction as we walked away with noses aloft, feigning considerable umbrage, before wandering down below the sports field to hold odd little pidgin English and play-acted communications with the always attendant group of barefoot, pitifully ragged, eternally hungry waifs from the hillside shacks and passing over whatever food or sweets and chocolate we could acquire from the canteen or NAAFI, and be invariably left with a distinct impression of the incalculable benefits and comparable luxury of our own upbringing, when some of these poor wretches had probably experienced the terrible fires of Christmas 1953 when 53,000 of them were rendered homeless, leaving the government with the colossal dilemma of somehow providing food and shelter and no alternative but to begin immediately the provision of massive blocks of utilitarian concrete housing, though the overwhelming volume of immigrants meant the problem remained into the 1960s.

Understandably, any daytime duty-free hours were at first enthusiastically spent away from the restrictions of camp life visiting the must-see (at least once) well-established places of interest such as the Peak Railway, with its wide-bodied railcars, and the chance to sit in the hilltop restaurant and view in wonderful seclusion the incomparable panoramic views of the colony above the unholy clamour created below, or wander around Tiger Balm Gardens built in 1935 by the legendary cure-all potion tycoon Aw Boon Haw, high above the sweep of Causeway Bay, at a cost of sixteen million HK dollars, and marvel at its seven and a half acre site bristling with elaborate stairways connecting the various hillside levels littered with huge strangely interpreted concrete animals in impossible poses, exuberantly ornamented, brilliantly colourful pagodas, menacing carvings of obscure religious deities and its over-indulgently terraced, garishly decorated, red-tiled centrepiece, the Haw Par mansion crowning the whole crazy cross between J.

Randolph Hearst's Xanadu and Disneyland like some unrestrained Hollywood interpretation of oriental architecture, while away on the northern slope of Victoria Peak the Botanic Garden provided an appreciated opportunity to sit and escape the pell-mell rush of the city below, which even those of a not particularly philosophical disposition occasionally appreciated.

Naturally, the deciding factor as to what proportion of our spare time was actually spent down in the city intent upon visits to the cinemas, the big armed forces clubs, or simply indulging in a few ice-cold beers followed by a visit to the Chanticleer bakery and shop on Nathan Road to finish off the evening with the luxury of one of their hug-beautifully crisp, heavily buttered hot ham rolls, or remain stuck in the billet resentfully bewailing dollar-less pockets, an all too frequent occurrence on any day after Saturday due to the British Army's miserable rates of pay, which even with the so-called overseas allowances never provided anywhere near an amount comparable to civilian rates or one conducive to the realisation of even the modest social expectations of a bunch of not exactly extravagant, mostly working-class lads, particularly once the cost of the one hundred and one personal items we were expected to purchase had been met, but then everyone who ever served in Her Majesty's armed forces was only too aware that the scrooges in Whitehall, who decided such impositions on their closely guarded accounts, appreciated and exploited the fact that while ever National Service continued, the cost of its upkeep provided the ideal excuse for strictly controlling the rates of pay while sanctimoniously endorsing the general over-moralistic attitude of the time in claiming that the more young men had in their pockets the more likely they were to get into trouble, although as a short-term regular I was in a slightly less deprived financial position than those struggling on a National Serviceman's miserly emolument.

It was, of course, all just one more example of the deplorably unjustified and outdated attitude of extreme and devious paternalism still being perpetrated at that time, in which those so defiantly decided as being eligible and suitably able to protect and all too often give their lives in sacrifice to their worldwide sticky-fingered little empires were not really regarded as being capable of deciding with any degree of responsibility what the fiscal priorities were for a few extra bloody shillings.

It was in reality a far greater bone of contention within the armed forces at that time than anyone had the courage to confront, and we were without doubt ridiculously underpaid when compared to the majority of armed forces, none of which bore a comparable responsibility to the constant and irksome undertaking to police a quarter of the world's population, and of course when compared monetarily to our always loaded and invariably crass Atlantic cousins, who poured into the colony to almost outnumber us, we were paupers and often reminded of it by them.

Of course, with the colossal amount of investment Washington had poured into the colony during and since the Korean War, it could quite reasonably be asserted that they were entitled to regard Hong Kong as almost on a par with Hawaii; certainly they exerted far more influence than Whitehall was capable of when it came to any question of the colony's dealings with the Chinese Mainland and comes as no surprise to anyone who experienced the situation then that even today, the Hong Kong dollar is still tied to its American equivalent, while what is not so obviously common knowledge is the fact that but for a splendid piece of opportunism executed in the best traditions of the British Empire by an unsung hero at the end of the Second World War, the Americans had been quite prepared to hand the colony over to their barmy old pet warlord Chiang Kai Shek when the Japanese surrendered.[1]

The 25th Field Regiment Royal Artillery had periodically since 1950 maintained one of its three component batteries of 25pdrs in

[1] Franklin Gimson arrived in the colony to take up the post of Colonial Secretary to the Governor Sir Mark Young on the day of the Japanese invasion and during his subsequent imprisonment in Stanley Camp as senior official internee implacably ensured that whenever possible the appearance of a functioning British Government in Hong Kong was upheld even to the extent of resisting all British civilian repatriations on the grounds that it would prejudice the colony's status after the war.

Malaya, providing support for the combined Commonwealth infantry regiments opposing the Communist uprising, which began in 1948, with 54 Battery there in 1950 and 93 Battery stationed there since 1952, so it came as no great surprise, though hardly welcomed, that rumours began to circulate around the camp that the regiment would soon be stationed there as a whole, but of course in keeping with most things the army plans, the orders to prepare to embark for Malaya went through more than one stage of assuredness, and last-minute cancellations were punctuated with frenzied last-minute training, inspections and the chance of a mid-morning trip out across the indefatigable bay on a courtesy visit towards the forty-five thousand tonne monumental grey immensity of the visiting American aircraft carrier USS *Midway* and bumping to a halt beneath its towering deck overhang before climbing skywards up the steep steel stairway in best battledress uniform and polished boots to ceremoniously salute the awaiting officer of the watch and then, as we had been previously instructed, assiduously turn to face and salute the huge stern-hung American flag, a punctilious piece of protocol which was rather reluctantly entered into without any great sense of transatlantic charity by most of our party, but on the other hand was doubtlessly relished by those occasional members of the crew who left us in little doubt as to their anti-Limey sympathies, but who at least demonstrated an ability to recognise who and what we were, unlike the more typically crass example of Okie, who escorted us around the immense deck areas packed with a surprisingly tatty-looking jet and conventional prop aircraft and who, to our bemused displeasure, immediately assumed that our wearing of the traditional black beret signified we were French.

When news of Japan's eventual surrender reached the camp on August 16th 1945, and with Sir Mark Young having been moved by the Japanese to Manchuria, Gimson immediately declared himself Acting Governor and representative of his Majesty King George VI in Hong Kong. Eleven days later a message from London granted him official authorisation.

His incentive action no doubt changed the course of history, it having been previously agreed by the Allied Powers that all liberated territories should be surrendered to whoever liberated them, and with no one having liberated the Crown Colony, logic suggested that it should be surrendered to the Supreme Commander of the war zone in which it was situated, i.e. the Nationalist warlord Chiang Kai Shek, who had long disputed the legality of Britain's presence and was backed by a distinctly colonially antagonistic America.

Gimson's initiative, however, had luckily created a *fait accompli* that even Washington was reluctant to reverse, so the Japanese formally surrendered Hong Kong to Admiral Sir Cecil Harcourt RN and thus ensured its continuation as a Crown Colony.

12. Moving On, 1955

With the confirmation of our impending move to Malaya having finally dispelled all the inevitable initial variation of rumours, which at one point by their abundance would have made any meeting of the Women's Institute envious, so began the Quartermaster's blood pressure bursting great inventory of equipment and stores, some of which, had they ever existed, appeared to have been mysteriously mislaid, or more likely surreptitiously disappeared long ago into the great material vacuum that was Hong Kong's interpretation of a black market, as we prepared to vacate Gun Club Barracks and forever be deprived of its suddenly appreciated amenities, its excellent NAAFI, its on-tap tailors, dhobi wallahs, suit pressers and the little old lady who seemed to be a permanent daytime presence squatting at one end of the billet incessantly darning socks and consequently moved into temporary residence in a pre-war erected leaky wooden hutted and canvas tent augmented transit camp situated on a piece of land isolated from the bustle of Chatham Road by a three-foot paling fence and backed by the clang, bang, whistle and throb of the Kowloon–Canton Railway.

Then, having despatched our 25pdr artillery pieces, transport and main equipment into the care of an advance party of some of the more senior members of 35 and 54 Batteries to Singapore on one of the big Landing Ship Transports, we all embarked on the troopship *Empire Fowey* on 6th April and regrettably left the colony, and spent the next three days below deck sweltering on lines of iron-hard bunk beds and gasping for air from the minute air vents in claustrophobic battery hen-like troop deck accommodation, while the single-funnel ex-German passenger ship, formerly named Potsdam, and one more of those end of the Second World War appropriations, conveyed us towards our second encounter with Singapore and ultimately our destination somewhere in Malaya.

During the early hours of the third day, the long, low all-white Fowey passed between the far distant shorelines of Indo-China and Borneo to eventually slide into Keppel Harbour, Singapore, opposite the small island of Blakang Mati to dock mid-morning in the vast grey vessel-crowded Empire naval dockyard, and we disembarked into the glaringly clear sunshine but humid temperature amid chaotic scenes of frantic activity, as gangs of Chinese labourers scurried beside the ageing trooper, pushing, pulling and, no doubt given the opportunity, pilfering, and almost certainly swearing over the piles of MOD boxes, crates and equipment swung from deck to quayside on lurching high derrick cranes, and hurriedly packed them onto the backs of a line of awaiting QM trucks, watched by a group of lounging army drivers, as we clambered into identical transport and, with an anticipated dedication to discomfort, were energetically bounced on the slatted seats through one of the main gates and across into the palm tree lined, smart black and white bungalow dotted avenue of Sembawang Road, and up along the dense vegetation-crowded roadway to pass the great MacRitchie, Pierce and Seletar reservoirs before entering the usual unmistakeable regimented configuration of large white concrete military buildings, wide parade ground and rows of atap-roofed corrugated sheet-sided bashas of Nee Soon garrison and Transit camp, to spend the next five days being relieved of our heavy UK-type battledress, although retaining the big clumsy ammunition boots; after all, among all the wonderfully dhobi-wallah wash and go informality of future drab olive-green 'jungle gear' and dark-green webbing, it was to the army imperative that we had something to polish.

We were afforded no opportunity throughout our short stay at Nee Soon to appreciate the camp's cinema, swimming pool or NAAFI, reacquaint ourselves with the delights of downtown Singapore's abundance of facilities, or even be tempted towards the depths of iniquity by the permanent encampment of often indefinable-gendered Indian, Malay and Chinese prostitutes opposite the main gate, and we were most definitely confined to camp, with most of our time taken up by being equipped with small arms, tents and other equipment more suitable for the duties we were expected to perform up country, cursing over a jumble of tonnes of uncounted, unopened and sometimes unidentifiable stores or sweating on the vast MT park restoring the regimental colours (the guns) to their usual impeccable state of glossy green paintwork and burnished steel and brass, ensuring everything needed was packed and loaded into the bewildering array of compartments, trays and pockets on the quads, then listening nervously to descriptions of the procedures to be followed in the event of an ambush by terrorists during the four-day journey up to our new Battery headquarters in Taiping in the northern state of Perak.

What little spare time we had, which meant anytime during the evenings, was spent forcing down anti-malarial Paludrine tablets, big gagging lemon-flavoured salt tablets to counteract dehydration, downing gallons of sickly sweet orange juice and, whenever possible, lying in a state of near exhaustion on uncomfortable charpoys with the corrugated sides of the basha raised outward in an attempt to alleviate the oven-hot temperature generated by the day-long sun.

Each morning we strolled in glorious sunshine or chased to the canteen in welcome tropical downpours of cooling rain before the ever-returning heat removed any trace of it, to lay claim to large plates of overcooked eggs, bacon, beans and piles of toast, and at midday sniffed suspiciously but invariably devoured whatever concoction of Anglo-Asian cuisine the catering corps could imaginatively come up with and, during the heavily fragrant, soft breeze cooled evenings, squatted around the tiny oil stoves of the visiting Tamil char-wallahs with great mugs of heavily-sugared, condensed-milk-lightened, strong, dark tea and munched on endless thickly-sliced bread and chip 'banjos' while fighting off the persistently attracted attention of alarmingly large flying bugs, even larger and aggravatingly humming moths and listened to the constant cicada chorus and harsh 'urpping' of giant frogs in the monsoon run-off drains, until reluctantly retiring to the stuffy interior of exasperating mosquito nets to sleep, soaked in sweat.

'A' Troop's early-morning departure on the fifth day was accomplished with enough swank and pretentious posing by the Troop Commander in his jeep, the troop leader in the ungainly little Dingo scout car and the No.1's standing up through the hatch on top of the quads to satisfy even General Custer, and we rolled noisily away from the main Nee Soon MT park to head north, then west to join the main Bukit Timah Road and swing onto the long straight, much restored after its strategic partial destruction by the beleaguered British in 1941, functionalism of the Singapore-Johore Bahru Causeway to take in our first view of the exuberant greenery of Malaya waiting to engulf us on the opposite shoreline and suddenly felt a growing sense of unease and apprehension as to what we were likely to encounter, almost expecting some sort of instant ambush the moment we entered.

Certainly, we had precious little appreciation of what to realistically expect or too much of what would be expected of us, even by those leading us on, more engrossed in how heroic they thought they looked than any awareness that they provided a remarkably easy target to any opportunistic CT with a rifle and a spare clip of ammunition; not that we as mere gunners were any more appreciably protected, the steel doors of each quad behind which we, the (four) members of each gun crew, sat in line abreast ('A' Troop never did manage to achieve the requisite complement throughout our time in Malaya and had to supplement the crews by roping in the quad drivers or any other available untrained body), having been removed to facilitate our easy exit in the event of any attack, but which also left us decidedly exposed and morbidly speculating on the potential damage even a single round of ammunition could inflict if directed into the cramped interior.

Once across the causeway we immediately entered Johore Bahru and passed the railway station to make our way through the unimpressive outer limits, with their dingy, dust-hung roadside market stalls, open-drained, single-slab bridged, grimy-looking 'five foot' walkways, low canopied shop/house fronts and wooden-walled, rusting tin-roofed huts half-hidden along well-worn pathway-divided strips of cultivation, ominously backed by uninviting scrub, a few rubber trees and eventual thick, dark jungle, before settling to roll along, gripping our unloaded short-barrelled Lee Enfield rifles as if the total Malay People's Liberation Army was waiting specifically for our trundling old Morris tractor, ammunition limber and gun, and praying silently that our example of the ugly old heap of outdated unarmoured arse-numbing discomfort wouldn't perform with their occasional bloody-mindedness and grind to a halt with the usual resigned and ridiculous radiator gurgle, at least until we reached some semblance of civilisation, a probability which seemed to become increasingly unlikely as we stared out at mile upon mile of gloomily interiored, regimented rubber tree plantations, impenetrable secondary jungle or dense swathes of tall lalang grass reaching to the road's edge, while at the more excessively sharp bends in the road dramatically conspicuous burnt-out cars had been dumped at the roadside, which were, not entirely convincingly, explained away as being purposely positioned hopefully effective remedials to the locals' fundamentally fatalistic incompetence as drivers and not the result of some past ambush.

Then, just as we had begun to relax slightly and no longer searched every piece of passing greenery quite so intently for anyone lurking about with a red star on his forage cap, our No.1 popped back into the quad interior from his standing position at the observation hatch and screamed out "Dismount and assume ambush positions!" and the limber and gun lurched violently forward in response to the driver's instant braking, causing the quad to skid forward a further two yards before it all came to a halt seconds after we had tumbled from the cab, hurling ourselves into the undergrowth, and found ourselves rolling down a steep embankment to slither into a shallow stagnant rainwater filled ditch, only to realise that every round of 303 ammunition was still neatly packed into one of the cab's locker compartments, a precaution insisted upon to prevent any trigger-happy idiot banging off at nothing in particular, the presumption being that one of us would remember to grab it before vacating the cab.

We emerged from our hideout ten minutes later and clambered back up to the road under bellowed instructions from Troop Sergeant Kelly, who was stalking up and down the length of the convoy waving the thick mahogany stick he was seldom seen without, informing everyone this had just been a rehearsal and obviously intended to ascertain how we would react, and judging from the 'about to explode' scarlet colour of his face, and the fact that he continually referred to us all as "useless bastards", we knew he was not in the least impressed by our performance, and abruptly marched off leaving us to return to our seats to sit slumped, with lacerated arms and itching bodies, our once well-starched uniforms now caked in mud and slime and exuding an aroma reminiscent of a Hong Kong smallholder's dung bucket, and with our essentially pessimistic regard for all things military satisfyingly reinforced, we continued the journey, struggling out of the stinking OGs and each sitting half naked and speechless within his own varying sense of humiliation, until a few miles on the driver momentarily lost concentration while attempting to pass one of the plodding water buffalo drawn carts we occasionally encountered and misjudged the clearance needed just sufficiently to cause the contraption to lurch sideways violently and propel the wizened old Malay in charge into a graceful upward trajectory and down into hopefully soft vegetation, while the great ugly buffalo awkwardly regained its balance and thundered on in our wake, to leave us with our squaddies' habitual appreciation for the humour in anyone's misfortune other than our own, screaming with laughter.

At around 10am we were far enough beyond our starting point to break open the supply of oversized cookhouse sandwiches intended to sustain us up to the town of Kluang, where we were to stop overnight to allow the vehicles and equipment to be checked and maintained, the sandwiches being consumed on the move by the expedient of whoever sat on the two innermost positions eating first while the two in the outer positions kept guard, presumably to prevent any starving CT jumping aboard and stealing the sandwiches, then simply changing positions, while the No.1 sat in his single seat beside the driver to enjoy his, and the poor driver was left to juggle with his while continuing to drive, all of which produced the usual issue of moans, complaints and oaths before abruptly turning to cheers and giggles when one of the parcels was clumsily fumbled and deposited to splatter in all its over-margarined sogginess in the middle of the road and provoke much semi-serious debate as to whether we could be charged with potentially supplying a squad of terrorists with enough food for the next two months.

With midday approaching and the box-like cab's constant exposure to the sun at its fiercest, combined with the heat from the engine continually reflecting back inside, the conditions in the cab were becoming unbearable, even minus the doors and with the observation hatch wide open, and the speed of the convoy just could not generate sufficient airflow to cool things down, so having perfunctorily debated the choice and odds of dying of dehydration, or some CT being a good enough marksman to hit an exposed head, we decided to take it in turns to stand with our heads poking out of the observation hatch to gulp in some relatively cooler air, while the driver, being in the worst possible position and persistently complaining his legs 'were on fire', eventually managed to perform an admirable feat of dual contortionism with the only other member of the crew capable of driving the rig, and without any inconvenience to the rest of the convoy as we chugged along until the crossroads at Ayer Hitam appeared and the long line of vehicles and equipment veered right to make the final pull up into the rubber plantation covered undulating hillsides surrounding the town and military base at Kluang, having taken a total of eleven hours to complete the seventy miles from Nee Soon.

When we crossed over the deep brown Mengibol River into Kluang, the whole town was alive with activity, and with the majority of its inhabitants dressed in olive-green uniforms and seemingly representing a pretty good cross-section of the British and Commonwealth and Malay Federation armies, from the RASC to REME, RAMC to Gurkhas and various unrecognisable units, our orders were to bunk down near to the 13 Infantry Workshops so that they could sort out a few of the problems the convoy was experiencing with the ever-demanding quad tractors, and for once found it almost pleasant to busy ourselves beneath the shade of overhead palms cleaning away the rod dust and removing the thick layer of bugs from the guns and limbers before polishing them up, and even better to guzzle down a few bottles of cool beer before spending the rest of the evening in the smoke-filled Army Kinema Corp bug-hut watching Lucille Ball and Desi Arnez in 'The Long Trailer', which in view of our recent experience over the previous eleven hours did seem suspiciously coincidental and caused the more sceptical of us to speculate whether some smart bugger had got the film in purposely.

The convoy made its way back down to the Ayer Hitam crossroads at first light next morning and headed north through the flood-prone typical, small, slightly scruffy Malay towns of Segamat and Gemas to then turn west down towards yet another army-based town, Tampin, where our sister Battery 93 Le Cateau had their headquarters, and who, despite being regarded throughout the rank and file of the rest of the regiment as a bunch of egotistical pain in the arses, who actually subscribed to all the elitist unit crap simply because they had been in Malaya longer than the rest of us, it came as something of a disappointment to find we were making an overnight stop to enable the officers to conduct the customary courtesy visit and conveniently flood themselves with cocktails, before we steamed on the next day to the small capital of the state of Negri Sembilan, Seremban, which sat beside the main railway line running up the eastern side of the country from the junction at Gemas, where the stretch from Singapore junctioned to split and allow one line to continue almost centrally, then eventually veering across to Kota Bharu and up the west coast and into Siam.

We, however, drove on, paralleling the west coast line and enduring one or two more of the ambush alarms, which ranged from genuine exercises to some stupid slightly inebriated officers' idea of a 'prank', before being involved in and delayed by a traffic accident, which the English superintendent of the civil police most generously decided "was not necessarily our fault", even if the wide-open roadways did at times seem to intoxicate our drivers into even more than usual questionable standards of manipulating the long snaking combination of quads, limbers and guns, though thankfully we were spared the possible nightmare of trying to negotiate the more complicated road system and traffic volume of the bustling capital of Malaya, Kuala Lumpur, and skirted round it to grind to a halt twenty miles further on for a day of rest at Kuala Kuba Bahru on the 18th of April.

The day of 'rest' rubbish was of course no more than a military euphemism for scrubbing, scraping and scouring everything at hand, before hammering down as many bottles of Tiger as we could cram into what little time there was left.

Next day we avoided the impressive Gothic, Moorish and Chinese architecturally influenced capital of the rich tin-mining state of Perak, Ipoh, and wound our way round to the Sultan of Perak's royal town of Kuala Kangsar, sitting in all its exquisite splendour just downstream of the great Kangsar River and thankfully, finally entered our destination, Taiping, hours before schedule to marvel at the high cloud-capped blue-tinted jungle-covered backdrop of Maxwell Hill for an arrival at our future Battery Headquarters the old Klian Pau convent and a reception, which could not have engendered less enthusiasm from the advance party already there had we brought back the whole Japanese army.

The Old Convent – we never referred to it as anything else by name, while reserving rather more colourful descriptive definitions for its disgusting initial impression – had lain derelict for so long it was quite surprising the destructive forces of the area's climatic humidity, proliferation of creepy crawlies and dreadful daily monsoon rainfall had not reduced it to a pile of sawdust and crumbling brickwork long before some gold braid over-laden clown sitting in his electric fan-cooled office somewhere wherever the Far East Land Forces HQ was described it as "slightly scruffy", and decided its remains would provide reasonable HQ admin and accommodation facilities for 35 Field Battery Royal Artillery, with a reassurance that there were plans to renovate it, but with its gaping roof and disintegrating wooden-boarded upper floor, piles of rat-infested rubbish-littered rooms and large concrete outside area in danger of disappearing under the intrusion of thick lalang grass and invasive vines, struck us as being the most disgustingly filthy hovel we had experienced since our occasional security patrols into the squatter shacks of Kowloon.

Luckily, the advance party had cleared enough space for us to park our vehicles and the guns before we offloaded everything we needed and were then directed to our slum-like accommodation on the ground floor, the upper floor being designated as completely unsafe, and it was only with a good deal of improvisation and invention as to cooking and other facilities that we managed to eke some degree of very basic existence and military order among the complete chaos during that first week as we went through the inevitable and of course imperative equipment checks, ensuring we were in possession of sufficient ammunition for personal weapons and enough shells and cartridges for the guns, listening to lectures by anyone who had any experience of operating artillery out in the Malay hinterland, being continually instructed on the general conditions and requirements of entering what would be our first experience of active service and hoping we were ready for whatever was to come, after which we were free to have a wander around the town and acquaint ourselves with whomever and whatever experiences we could dig up among its wide tree-divided avenues, shabby connecting grimy-walled banner-hung alleyways, cramped unkempt bars, smoky squaddie-filled cinemas showing old musicals and hardly reassuring news items about the anti-terrorist operations being conducted all around us, the inevitable complement of young prostitutes hanging around anywhere there was a soldier, plenty of opium-smoking old men glimpsed in dismal back rooms and marvelling at the amazing pile specialists' premises discovered on Tupai Road, with its lobby walls hung with explicit portraits of haemorrhoid-afflicted derrieres.

Not that Taiping lacked more intrinsically appreciable attractions; it was beyond the inelegant confines of its main town limits, unarguably set among some of the most breathtakingly beautiful country in all Malaya, where great sweeps of eye-achingly intense rainforest circled around and above it to overlay every incline and hollow with the luxurious exuberance of vegetation guaranteed by its unfailing daily downpour of warm tropical rain and the resultant steamy humidity, which would cause us so many health alarms and problems by inflicting the weird and disquieting roll call of skin diseases from Tinea, with its violent outbreaks of fiery rashes, the maddeningly exquisite itching eruptions of extreme athlete's foot, to frightening between-the-toes burrowings of heaven knows what parasite, and minute airborne insects that landed on even the smallest area of exposed anatomy to gorge on blood and then fall off like miniscule vampires, and all this in addition to the ever-present irritation and hazards of mosquitoes and leeches.

Of course, with medical facilities available at BHQ Taiping all this was largely controllable, and sick parades, periodic skin examinations and a strict regime of anti-malaria tablets, plus common sense, ensured most complications were kept surprisingly minimal, with even those who chose to disregard the continually emphasised threat of court martial, and risked contracting something very unpleasant by employing the services of the local trishaw transported 'Taggies', were catered for with available supplies of free condoms and a town centre, medical orderly staffed, post-indulgence treatment kiosk, though, having once been the recipient of the ex-Japanese prisoner of war, Battery Sergeant Major's incontestable wisdom during a conversation outside the QM stores, as he nonchalantly pulled the ends off a box of army issue condoms and exclaimed, "Nothing lasts here, boy, it's the bloody climate, rots everything!" was quite enough to deter me from the temptation to disregard my mother's final instruction before my embarkation, "and keep yourself clean".

On 23rd April we of 'A' Troop coupled up the four guns and limbers to the quads and, accompanied by our transport complement of one jeep, one QA three tonner, one ancient 15cwt signals and technical assistants' truck and a Dingo scout car, drove away from Taiping heading west to Sungei Siput, the small northern Perak tin-mining town twenty miles from the Elphil rubber estate, where the long drawn-out political saga of Communist rebellion had originally erupted into violent confrontation on the 16th of June 1948 with the murder of the plantation manager Arthur Walker by three Chinese Communists and the subsequent killing of John Allison, another estate manager, and his assistant Ian Christian, during a raid by twelve terrorists on the same day, and resulted in Perak eventually achieving notoriety as being second only to the state of Johore as the most terrorist active state in Malaya.

Sungei Siput itself was a typical Chinese/Malay small town with a very wide, usually almost motor free main street divided by a line of miserable-looking trees down the centre and flanked by the inevitable shallow monsoon drains occasionally bridged by flat slabs to allow access to the rows of gloomy shops/houses, eating places and a drab, tacky cinema, which continually showed the screechy Cantonese or wailing over-acted Indian musicals aimed at the two races who provided the majority of labour in the area and easily outnumbered the indigenous Malays, and all of which conveyed that seedy rundown air that we were to become so familiar with.

Behind this apathetic display of civilisation, the town dissolved into a few lines of rubber trees and scrub, where a good many of the mine labourers and peasants lived in tin shack and tarpaulin huts, while beyond the curfew-ensuring surrounding high-wire fence and food-check controlled gated entrance lay a mixture of dense jungle and open scars of exhausted and abandoned opencast tin mines (Tailings) and monsoon-filled dredging pools, their edges spotted with sparse vegetation, which all helped to create an impression of ugly oases in small incongruously sited deserts, one of which was to be the base for our first participation in anti-terrorist operations, and which, on our turning off from the narrow secondary road to bump down a small track and splash through the muddy water of a wide stream onto the mechanically flattened open area of the old workings, imparted the immediate impression of having more evident potential for filming some 'B' movie, Western or French Foreign Legion epic than any apparent advantage for any kind of home to 'A' troop, and we pulled up in a cloud of dust, half expecting to be instructed to circle the wagons, but instead, after rolling out the four artillery pieces into their designated positions, lined the transport up and set to erecting the ridge tents that would be our accommodation, and the large canvas cookhouse and eating area, then augured the all-important hole in the ground ready to be crowned with a brand new single-seater thunderbox, itself surrounded on three sides by a hessian sheet in deference to modesty way down at the outer limit of the area by the surrounding sagging wire fence, a location of sufficient solitude to ensure a degree of privacy and also guarantee it being the one destination to which its frequent patrons never forgot the now insisted upon directive to carry small arms at all times, no one understandingly relishing the quite conceivable prospect of being shot at in such unacceptably embarrassing circumstances without at least having the option of returning fire.

On two sides of the immediate area of the new gun position the mixed topsoil and ochre and umber coloured sand from past excavations had been piled up haphazardly like surrounding monsoon-gouged, sparsely vegetated modest hillsides, while to the west the eerie spectacle of far distant greenery clustered outcrops rose in towering hazy silhouette, at times brilliantly illuminated by intense beams of sunlight emanating through angrily rolling rainclouds scudding across what appeared to be a wide savannah-like foreground, but was, in reality, no more than the overgrown exhausted remains of yet more alluvial opencast tin mining immediately beyond the limit of our position.

To the east, the outlook changed yet again, with the rainforest creeping threateningly towards us on high hillsides and deep valleys before petering out, held by the gradual dearth of topsoil and the lack of the forest's nutrient-rich requirement, leaving only sparse patches of indefatigable scrub and determinably assertive grasses edging forward to the exposed expanse of featureless sand, upon which, had we the slightest inclination to appreciate its possible effectiveness as an artillery firing site, with daytime temperatures at a constant eighty degrees plus, the usual Malaya humidity of around ninety and the only effective shade being our ridge tents or the canvas sheet erected over the few tables and chairs which constituted the dining area as the home for around thirty personnel, it seemed particularly ironic that we who had left the relative luxury of Hong Kong for a continent supposedly defined by its gigantic monsoon-fed jungles, should now find themselves plonked on a dry and dusty sun-baked mini Sahara, while our already less than appreciative opinion of the organisational ability and commitment of the commissioned clowns supposedly in charge of us was compounded further by the realisation that their concern for our welfare and comfort hadn't even extended to providing us with a few camp beds, they of course being of a more genteel upbringing having previously ensured their own, while we were expected to doss down on the ground inside our mosquito nets, with the edges tucked under our groundsheet, a prospect which may well have appealed to their Boy Scout mentality or perhaps simply compounded their personal prejudices, but which left for us a lot to be desired as a position to retire to after spending each day pouring with sweat from humping heavy ammunition, banging away on cordite-stinking smoky-hot guns and engaging in the many guard duties and other bits of nonsense they could drum up to fill our time with.

It eventually took an initiative from the TSM to rectify the unsatisfactory situation by the simple expedient of despatching the QA truck with a scrounging party to beg, steal or borrow a load of old scrap wood and signal wire for each man to construct his own interpretation of the ideal divan.

In the meantime, we had settled into a routine which entailed painstakingly scrubbing out the interior of the gun barrels with boiling water, then drying and polishing the rifling with the big rope pull-throughs, before religiously greasing and oiling the recoil system after each day of feverishly blasting away with high explosive at whatever target we were given in an attempt to accomplish whatever we were supposed to be doing to the CTs, which, according to the infantry, who rather ungraciously always refused to appreciate our efforts, was usually little more than causing the terrorists to pack their bags and move to a new location, possibly nursing a few headaches.

In the main, our other most important duty consisted of maintaining guard throughout the long nights, when our immediate surroundings were so abruptly transformed from the unambiguous clarity of bright openness to the imposition of an almost claustrophobic, deceptively shape-and-shadow filled semi-darkness of dusk before night brought its never quite complete silence, unnervingly disturbed with curiously perplexing howls, squeals and snorts, and the slightest pinpoint glow or sharp transmission of light served to quicken the senses and heighten the always present suspicion that we could be under surveillance by CTs from most points around our only too accessible position, and until we gradually grew accustomed to its peculiar eeriness and came to terms with our own constant sense of insecurity, caused more than one jittery individual to sound general alarm and result in other members of the guard awaiting the opening fusillade of shots from our imagined assailants, only to discover the cause of all the panic was no more than a gathering of amorous fireflies, or some idiot wandering around the distant jungle with an oil lamp, in which case this being in contravention of the curfew regulations, a burst from a Bren gun in the general direction of the offender usually ensured an instantaneous solution to the problem.

A necessary consideration, other than trying to improve our living conditions as much as we could within what was practical and permissible while exiled on our ecological eyesore, which didn't leave us with much choice, was that of creating some sort of alternative focus during our few off-duty hours other than continually getting plastered on never cold enough Tiger beer, just to end up wistfully mooning on about 'back home', plus contending with a troop commander, whose only answer to any question regarding the maintenance of morale never achieved any degree of imagination beyond introducing additional duties or operations, some of which did thankfully now and then at least create the opportunity to couple up a single gun and limber and move out of camp as a 'roving gun' to wander down some side road and bang off a few rounds at whatever target was available, or find ourselves farmed out to provide additional help, or hindrance, to the Malay police personnel at the local kampongs (villages), who had the essential job of enforcing the curfew and searching any civilians leaving the compound between the hours of 7am and 7pm and who may be tempted or coerced into attempting to smuggle out small quantities of food to the terrorists.

We, however, decided our emotional needs required the introduction of something upon which we could possibly focus our affections, and so acquired the first of our troop mascots, a small black and tan dog of indefinable pedigree, probably best described as a long-legged version of a Jack Russell terrier, which, from the very first day of its recruitment, was universally accepted, unremittingly pampered, totally undisciplined and left to wander around the gun site passing the time of day with whoever was available, being continually fed with the most inappropriate food, lying motionless under a vehicle when the midday heat became unbearable or disappearing without trace when the guns were blasting out HE or smoke shells, that is until a second pet was introduced, whereupon the poor mutt's existence, and ours, changed considerably.

When the long-tailed Macaque monkey first arrived it was no more than a minute bag of bones with elongated limbs and a tiny head, and initially elicited even more sympathetic approval than the dog, though how it was acquired remained forever known only to the troop ACC cook, who brought it back after one of his stock-up food trips to No.2 RASC Supply Depot in Taiping, which was where the Gurkhas obtained imported live sheep and goats as part of their diet and gave rise to the more vociferous critics of the cook's culinary expertise by suggesting the ape had originally been intended as a rather exotic supplement to one of his invariably monotonously unimaginative stews, while what none of us realised during those early days of lavishing affection upon the little creature was that that particular type of monkey has a natural predilection for mischievousness, but that was something that soon became increasingly obvious with the beast's instinctive recognition of the potential for creating mayhem by mercilessly irritating the poor dog into a state of howling helpless frustration by endlessly teasing it and pelting it with any available missiles from some convenient out-of-reach vantage point, or inflicted the ultimate humiliation by suddenly materialising to leap on the pup's back like some demented rodeo rider until the maddening assault upon his canine dignity was terminated by a frenzied dash beneath the tables and chairs in the dining area, leaving the dog to flee in desperation far to the outer limits of the camp.

All this of course provided us with some welcome moments of hilarity at a time when the epitome of fun unerringly seemed to depend solely upon how far some of us were prepared to accept looking like complete idiots while under the influence of too much Tiger beer, though our appreciation of the monkey's antics began to quickly dissipate when it began to develop a nocturnal habit of suddenly flying through the tent entrance flaps to crash land onto the mosquito net of whoever happened to be lying beneath, all of which, once the comic potential began to pall among the ever-increasing toll of targets, inevitably resulted in a unanimous decision to curtail its after-dark escapades by restraining it each evening with a very light chain fastened to a steel pole, from which flew the regimental flag and from where the forlorn-looking hapless ape watched with large accusatory eyes until we discovered his pitiful body one morning, chain wrapped, hanging from the post like some tiny crucified martyr.

Shortly after we had taken up residence on the Sungei gun site, a troop of the 1st Singapore Regiment of Artillery arrived in a great cloud of dust dragging two huge 3.7-inch anti-aircraft guns with massive Matador transporters and set up camp further down the spacious tailings by a large dredging pool.

Nicknamed the Blakang Mati cowboys in recognition of their home base on the small island at the entrance to the harbour of Singapore and their smart Gurkha-type headgear, and contrary to the sardonic observation of one of our members that the role of the 3.7s would probably be to protect us from any overhead attack by the aircraft of the terrorist air force, which, notwithstanding the fact that it was an entirely fictitious unit, would have possibly accounted for the fact that they never actually fired from Sungei, though they did memorably venture out into the Perak countryside one day to apparently accidently roll a gun irretrievably down into a ravine, and the unit's British officers seemed to spend an inordinate amount of time each day sitting in the shade and downing copious amounts of gin while entertaining a continual parade of eccentric-looking visitors, one of whom was instrumental in providing a rather bizarre event which at least helped to lighten one of the boringly indistinguishable days of our existence, and which began during one of the occasional opportunities to disport ourselves in the probably quite unhealthy pool of still water, which lacked even sufficient nutritional elements to support visible evidence of plant or animal life, but which quite possibly held many far more unhealthy traces disturbed during the original excavation of which we remained blithely unaware as we splashed and swam in our predominantly 'au natural' innocence, before realising that a long sun-bleached hair, sarong-draped female figure was making its slightly unsteady, obviously gin-impelled progress towards the pond, and on reaching the water's edge gazed around with unmistakable appreciation of all the open-mouthed individuals momentarily transfixed by her unexpected appearance, before grasping the securing fold of her garment and allowing it to fall dramatically around her feet to reveal her still slim if less than youthful figure in all its potentially disruptive nakedness, and splashing past a frantically genital-covering Scots non-swimmer sitting in the shallows and plunging into the tepid water, to be enthusiastically accompanied around the pool in a quite touching exhibition of dubiously earnest concern for her safety by a couple of excited Cockneys, while the more modestly inhibited members of the bathing party vacated the waters with alacrity, stumbled up towards the tent lines and inadvertently alerted the Troop Commander, who instantly despatched his Irish wolfhound, the recently appointed replacement Troop Leader Lt 'Paddy' Burke to stand at the water's edge ordering us out, and being already aware of his own reputation for dalliances with fellow officers' wives, his intervention we knew was hardly likely to be in the interests of our moral welfare, but comply we did to leave our newly acquired and appreciated naked playmate and disgruntledly slouch away, muttering long and suitably derogatory epithets regarding the invalidity of his parentage.

13. Patrols, Holes & Food Checks, 1955

We left the gun position late that afternoon to bounce onto the narrow secondary jungle-lined asphalt road that led south to Chemor.

It was Able 1's turn to provide what had become known as the 'roving gun', which simply meant that on receipt of the daily Situation Report from the infantry, if the proposed target lay beyond the twelve-mile range of the guns from their position at Sungei Siput, a single gun would be towed out to the most accessible point at which we could engage the target, and with our usual mix of trained gunners, the unenthusiastically assisting quad driver and accompanied by an RA signaller and one Tara, who between them had responsibility for providing us with target coordinates, we set off, relieved to be escaping the repetitive monotony of daily camp routine for a few hours and the opportunity to at least look at different scenery beyond the mini-desert, and led by the Gun Position Officer 2nd Lt Kirkman, a gentleman who by his very languid demeanour had managed to so far evoke little more effective response than a tolerantly bemused indifference among those he was supposedly there to lead, motivate and inspire, which suited the majority of the members of the troop who were National Servicemen and primarily interested in achieving the completion of their term with the least amount of aggravation, but mistakenly gave little consideration to the always possible eventuality that at some point their own safety may depend on the effectiveness as a leader of the young man now swaying and bouncing in the observation hatch of the Bedford 15cwt transporting the boards, maps and equipment of the technical assistant plus the RA signaller with his bulky Type 62 signals set, we all, despite our ever-present recognition of the vulnerability of our position, appreciated the opportunity to be out and about.

Naturally being the army, these forays were never conducted entirely spontaneously, and usually involved someone venturing out as soon as possible and prior to the guns' departure to reconnoitre a suitable firing position, a duty on this occasion undertaken by the TC himself, whereby he marked the firing point by placing two large empty cooking-oil tins, which on our arrival at the map reference had been possibly appropriated by some passing oriental gentleman and probably utilised as part of his vegetable patch irrigation equipment, but being reasonably sure we had found the correct spot we duly uncoupled the gun and limber and manoeuvred them into position on the wide grass verge quite close to the strip of mixed rubber, palm trees and assorted undergrowth which lined most Malayan roadways, before assuming our usual lounging positions until the map references, angles, range and other data had been calculated by the officer and Tara, and we were told to "Take post" to quickly go through the procedure of adjusting the dial sight, elevation, level and direction that brought the barrel into the required position, and at which point in the proceedings instead of ordering us to load and fire, the officer decided to stroll across to the gun and crouched low over the trail, then leaned forward to peer inside the open empty breech and illuminate the barrel with a small torch before smiling sweetly, nodding sagely and muttering "That's fine" and sauntering back to the Tara's trestle table, leaving us to stare at each other in disbelief at his ridiculous assumption that looking up the barrel could establish anything more relevant than that the bloody thing was empty, and certainly sweet Fanny Adams as to the possible trajectory of the shell when fired, and demonstrating what we could only construe as his alarming lack of confidence in the coordinates he had just helped to formulate.

Still, ours was but to do and bugger it, so we shrugged our shoulders resignedly, and on the order loaded shell and cartridge, closed and clamped the breech before I, as gun-layer, then yanked the small brass firing handle, and we all heard the great 'crack' of ignition and experienced the immediate slam of the recoil, the usual 'whoosh' and cloud of white smoke blast from the muzzle vents as the shell exited the barrel, to be instantly followed by a great unfamiliar roar, an almighty 'clang' and a grinding metallic tearing sound, and to watch mesmerised as a huge shower of shredded foliage and splinters collapsed earthwards accompanied by much flapping of wings, noisy squawking's, howls and chattering as the birdlife and monkeys scarpered.

Then followed a second or two of total silence before a cacophony of shrieks, screams and terrible wailings emanated a short distance from within the plantation, and we, dumbfounded and slightly disorientated, stood rooted to the spot, until like some ridiculous background from a Goon radio show the clip-clop-clap of rubber sandals on asphalt was accompanied by a great many very, very angry voices as we waited for whatever was about to descend upon us, and the road erupted with a melee of distinctly aggravated Malays, all gabbling madly, waving fists and wildly gesturing in the general direction that we had despatched the solitary shell.

Of course there was little we could do but stand about with small arms ready, trying to look soldierly, while the officer, his customary nonchalance now visibly undermined by this sudden and unexpected confrontation, stood surrounded by raging Malays trying to decipher the exact cause of their grievance and vainly attempting to placate them by assuming just the sort of Sanders of the River type colonial benevolence likely to get him lynched, which hardly helped when we realised that we had successfully directed the shell through the upper part of one of their homes and removed a large part of its corrugated tin roof.

Two hours later we were still there, confronted by a few of the inconsolable arm-waving mob, all screeching their protests and for all we knew threatening us with everything from the usual claims for exorbitant reparations to death by a thousand Kris cuts, and we, growing increasingly brassed-off with the whole bloody cock-up, threatened among ourselves to shoot the next bastard who came near enough to breathe the appalling odours of his last meal of chilli and fish stew over us, while the officer and our unenthusiastic No.1, escorted by the majority of the Malays, went to view the crime scene.

The details of our ridiculous foul-up having preceded our return to Sungei by courtesy of the signaller, we arrived back to a mixture of ironically intentioned congratulations for having on this occasion achieved at least some positive evidence of results from our usually underestimated and unseen efforts, a good deal of sarcastic suggestion that it was our revenge for the loss of the two cooking-oil tins, a distinct absence of the slightest sympathetic consideration for the Malays involved, consequently facing a night praying to Allah that the rains would hold off, and precious little appreciation for the presumed position of the one person we knew ought to accept responsibility for the whole mess, but who, with the assistance of a not entirely surprising endeavour by the TC 'Pansy Potter' to save face and direct the greater part of the blame onto us silly buggers in the gun crew, was the next day summarily returned to Taiping along with our unfortunate No.1, where the incident was investigated fully by the Battery Commander, and the truth emerged with the result that we were completely exonerated, and the 2nd Lt was put out to pasture in a less potentially harmful administrative post, and the question of appropriate reparations for the damage caused was settled under the terms of the scurrilous agreement engineered by Whitehall and the rubber and tin-mining industries, whereby the whole shooting match was only ever throughout its twelve-year-long conduct designated as a civil emergency and not a full-scale guerrilla war precisely to enable those industries to recoup damages from the insurers Lloyds, and also in practice unfailingly served to exacerbate the deep sense of resentment felt by the forty thousand soldiers involved, most of whom were foregoing a significant part of their youth in opposing the MNLA and its supply organisation the 'Min Yuen', and in far too many instances unethically sacrificed.

A week later we acquired a replacement National Service officer, a typically uncomplicated young gentleman with all the requisite good manners and impressive accent guaranteed to ensure his acceptance in the Taiping BHQ recently completed officers' mess and assured him of a reasonably worry-free existence in the troop, and who proved just as ineffective at what he was really supposed to represent and achieve as the previous one.

Out beyond the southern section of wire that looped around the Sungei Siput gun position, and bulging incongruously, their intermittent bulk shrouded in veils of heat mist rising from the surrounding monsoon-soaked tree mass, towering scrub-encrusted limestone rock formations loomed with dramatic effect like immense foreboding natural fortifications, and it was in the direction of these that early one morning four of us from Able Troop accompanied a Gurkha patrol during one of our less actively operating periods to participate in what was intended to be one more opportunity for us humble artillerymen to at least experience some of the conditions, terrain and general operating difficulties encountered by the infantry during their day-to-day conduct of the guerrilla war rather than any specifically seriously offensive manoeuvre, though in Malaya the chance of any patrol meeting trouble always remained a distinct possibility.

Naturally, all the accepted and usual precautions, procedures and codes of dress still applied, with our group being armed in total with one shoulder-slung Bren gun and a length-reduced double-barrelled shotgun in addition to our everyday normal equipment of the small Lee Enfield No.5 Mk 1 rifle with waist-slung 303 ammunition bandolier or the much-hated Sten gun with belt-hung magazine carrier and a long-bladed machete.

We arrived at the chosen outcrop after a short lorry ride followed by much sweatily energetic slashing at tangles of vines, lalang and bamboo copses, diligently following the leading Gurkha Sergeant until he suddenly pushed his way into a patch of undergrowth directly at the base of the outcrop, then motioned us forward and indicated we were now about to enter what appeared to be a small hole in the limestone followed by an immediate drop of four feet to the interior floor level.

This we all accomplished by simply sliding to the edge and bumping awkwardly over, and dropping blindly and landing heavily with more than a twinge or two of apprehension as we shuffled forward into the blackness and sour-smelling atmosphere of the interior to accommodate those entering behind us, before, having adequately adjusted to the reduced light, setting off in single file, following the man in front as closely as was reassuringly practical and peering forward suspiciously into the dank claustrophobic tunnel, its smooth walls and intimidatingly low ceiling fleetingly visible under the waving beam of the Sergeant's torch.

Soon we reached what appeared to be an intersection and the commencement of a second passageway, which lay a further three feet below the level of the one we had just negotiated but this time ran with the first slow tricklings of an underground stream, and it was down into this that we clambered to continue the next stage of our subterranean hike towards the centre of the great rock formation, only to discover that the further we progressed the more obvious it became that the level of the stream was rising steadily, until we reached a point where we were having to push our way uncomfortably through the very clear cold water at thigh height and momentarily stop to remove the waist-slung ammunition bandoliers to drape and secure them around our necks, a rather complicated adjustment while still struggling to keep our weaponry dry and one that gave rise to one of our apprehensive party members muttering a slightly anxious enquiry as to whether anyone knew where the "f---!" we were going, which instantly received from the Sergeant the curt reprimand, "Soldier, no talk!", his low but authoritative voice slightly amplified by the now narrowing and increasingly low-ceilinged passageway, while to most of us, despite the physical discomfort of half crouching, slightly stumbling our way across the unseen unpredictable surface of the stream bed, it was already quite evident that this was really just one more incursion into a location the Gurkhas had visited many times during their eternal search for evidence of CT activity.

With wristwatches being one of the personal items, among many, definitely forbidden at the start of the trek, we had absolutely no appreciation of the passage of time as we burrowed ever deeper into the core of the great rock; certainly it seemed to take an age of splashing along the corridor in our cramped, constantly uncomfortably bent posture before we reached a point where the tunnel opened sufficiently to allow us to relax slightly, and the continuing unpleasant sensation of disorientation lessened to where our seemingly slow progress was more tolerable, before suddenly we were sliding awkwardly over the face of a small channel where the stream sluiced away diagonally and then disappeared noisily, gurgling into some even deeper recess of the cave system, and the Sergeant muttered, "Nearly there now, boys," and clambered up an opposite rising slope of tunnel for us to eagerly follow him into its inviting long, bright light-reflecting opening, our spirits noticeably raised at the prospect of success and the conclusion of at least part of our troglodyte experience as we sloshed and dripped our way a further hundred yards along to the tunnel's conclusion and filed out onto a wide rock rim to stand stunned by the sheer unexpected spectacle of the monumental cave that had opened up before us, it's great craggily terraced walls rising like the interior of some colossal natural cathedral, its jagged neck-craning top partially open to the sky and its brilliant dust-laden light alive with the tiny blurs of darting swifts as it descended to illuminate the greater area of the unevenly shelved dark shadowed floor, the whole extraordinary edifice immediately evoking childhood memories of exciting post-war bus trips with my parents to the great celebrated caverns of my father's native Derbyshire.

Soon we were making our way along a well-worn narrow winding pathway down to the cave's huge saucer-shaped base, there to stand together listening avidly as the Gurkha Sergeant pointed out the tell-tale signs of past CT occupation, a blackened shallow rock indentation filled with the ashes of previous fires, a shadow-hidden disintegrating piece of canvas shoe, a small smooth area of rock face scratched with Chinese symbols and lettering, perhaps recording some wistfully sad reference to a long-abandoned home or loved one, or possibly just recording the Chinese equivalent of 'Kilroy was here', while other pathetic evidence such as heavily rusting food tins, which, upon close examination, bore the unmistakeable marks of Second World War army issue rations, were in fact the infinitely more poignant remains and reminders of the final days of some wretchedly abandoned and demoralised remnants of a British or Commonwealth unit desperately hiding before eventual capture or surrender to the victorious Japanese army in 1941.

Later, we again formed up in single file and trooped out of the huge basin and into yet another dark, damp passageway, diligently following the Gurkha Sergeant and his men, but now only too aware and appreciative of the fact that we, in comparison to the cave's past occupants, had the irreplaceable privilege of freely vacating the intriguing, impressively majestic, but overwhelmingly melancholic reminder of the appalling sacrificial privations imposed upon and endured by too many young men during Malaya's not so recent past.

As part of a practice that probably reflected as much upon the perpetual imbalance existing in all armies between administrative and actual front-line troops than any particular suitability for the role, since the beginning of the Malayan Emergency, units of the Royal Artillery had in addition to their normal duties also been required to perform many of the tasks which would normally have come under the Infantry's responsibility, even at times to the extent where they found themselves in a total infantry role, the first of these being the 26th Field Regiment in 1947, well before the emergency had been officially declared, while our own 93 (Le Cateau) Battery, who were stationed in Tampin in Negri Sembilan State, had been partly operating as infantry since 1952, though they as a result unfortunately acquired a ridiculously arrogant elitist attitude towards the rest of the regiment which was very much resented, while we poor relations, who they regarded as 'Johnny come lately', in addition to our artillery role were also involved in an occasional foot patrol and often the more menial duties such as accompanying the Federation Police and Malay Home Guard in conducting kampong food checks and night patrols, a not exactly gratifying exercise which involved spending a few days and nights camped within the kampong compound and between the hours of 7am and 7pm helping in the search for possible secreted packages of rice or other foodstuffs when the big wire gates which restricted access along the main kampong roads were opened for the villagers to leave and pursue their work on the surrounding rubber plantations and smallholdings, with each morning invariably beginning with a crowd of bicycle-pushing rubber tappers in disgustingly smelly, latex-stiffened, raggedy shorts and shirts and black samfu-suited ladies yoke-carrying the even more evilly repellent large open-topped tins of diluted human excrement for the vegetable patch, all jostling to get through the restricted exit with all the impatience, which when it comes to a question of earning money, the Chinese are capable of, while we, being always rather less convinced than the Malay guards, who were predominantly anti-Chinese anyway, of the necessary gravity of a situation which possibly denied some poor soul sitting out in the jungle a few grains of rice, perfunctorily examined an occasional bicycle frame for signs of any obvious modifications or poked a long sliver of bamboo through the handlebars and very, very reluctantly dragged another rod around in the revolting crap containers, and questioned the sometimes large bundle of banknotes being carried out by the local businessman before handing him over to the police for interrogation.

Now and again we would be offered packets of cigarettes as a sweetener, but they being of the lung-bursting Chinese variety, no one professed the slightest interest in them, and once the morning melee was over we were free to retire to our tent and wash the lingering stink of latex and sweat off at the village well, then heat up a few tins of whatever on the small 'Tommy' solid fuel cooker before spending the rest of the afternoon lazing about or wandering around the area talking to the kids or appreciating the slim, dark-haired, always immaculately clean and tidy Chinese girls or the Malays in colourful sarongs, and then, when the almost instantaneous night fell, venturing forth to make periodic patrols through the town and among the scattering of rough huts tucked away among the inevitable rubber trees which lay behind most Perak villages, diligently searching for any obvious signs of damage to the eight-foot high wire, 'keep 'em in, keep 'em out' fence, a routine which always assumed a quite spooky aura when the only illumination was the glimmer of soft moonlight through the overhead canopy of foliage and the twinkling of yellow paraffin lamps escaping through the many knotholes in the rubber tappers' cabin sides, and which were occasionally utilised in pursuit of one of our more questionable pranks, in which we would silently approach a hut and observe the occupants through a knothole in the hope that some unsuspecting amorous couple might be pursuing what comes naturally, in which case we would wait patiently for the appropriate moment of passion, then hammer on the side of the hut with our rifle butts and watch the mosquito net covered figures catapult from the sleeping platform to land with agonised screeches in a heap on the floor, before we stole away into the darkness, knowing the unfortunate victims would be too terrified to dare to venture outside, and completely indifferent to the possibility we had probably just increased the determination of two more among the majority of Malaya's colonial subjects ever-more vociferously demanding 'Merdeka' (Freedom).

Naturally, there were other occasions when our very occasional lapses into behaviour less than appropriate for Her Britannic Majesty's representatives were quite justifiably offset by some result of our own incompetence, one of which was an embarrassing incident which also occurred during an after-dark patrol among the permanently morbidly gloomy patches of rubber trees and scrub vegetation behind Sungei Siputs grungy-looking, smelly street, with our four-man patrol padding as silently as possible along a narrow undergrowth-lined pathway nervously cradling our rifles and Sten guns in the 'ready to respond' position, when the lead man raised one arm and we froze dramatically, half-expecting to be immediately enfiladed with shot from an ambush, only for the lead man to point to a thick piece of scrub, quickly flick the safety catch of his rifle forward and fire a single round of 303 ammunition into the thicket, probably more in nervous reaction to his own heightened sense of apprehension than any realistic expectation of bagging himself the prize of some visitant CT, only to hear a terrible scream and see the bushes violently thrown apart as one of the town goats vaulted from its unassuming resting place to fall dead at his feet, though even this humiliating episode was rendered acceptably insignificant by the totally infantile endeavour of our perennially detested Lt 'Paddy' Burke, who managed to create a wonderfully inappropriate example of military responsibility to those of us he so conspicuously regarded with a complete lack of respect, when he was consequently confined to BMH Taiping after shooting himself in the foot with his own Webley pistol during a boozy juvenile game of cowboy quick-draw.

14. Things to do in Salak Bahru, 1955

After three months of optimistically lobbing high explosive into the Peak Jungle, it was decided that both we and our equipment were ready to be returned to BHQ Taiping to allow everything, including ourselves, to be cleaned up, away from the ever-present dust of the Sungei Siput position, and wherever necessary overhauled at two Infantry REME workshops or replaced, a move which would also afford us the welcome chance of a short period of rest and recuperation before our next outing, so to no one's regret we set about stripping the camp and loading everything into any and every available truck and trailer, then made a much-relieved pass through the town avenue before looping round and crossing the wide brown waters of the Perak River at the royal town of Kuala Kangsar, its always serene-appearing jumble of homes nestling into the great sand-banked curve of the river, majestically watched over from the summit of high landscaped knoll by the Sultans' great Art Deco palace Istana Iskandaria, before making a swing northwards to eventually enter Taiping past the long forbidding outer walls of the prison and finally grind to a halt through the entrance to the familiar Old Convent, and receive the Battery Sergeant Major's customary vitriolic welcome for anyone returning from up-country, from which, one might have imagined, we had just come back from spending a day picnicking on Maxwell Hill, and not just completed a prolonged period of discomfort existing under smelly canvas on home-made beds on a miserable misplaced semi-desert eating the appalling concoctions produced by two creatively unconcerned cooks, and relying on semi-stagnant, always tepid water from an inadequate tanker trailer for drinking and ablutions, not that he, nor indeed many at BHQ above the rank of sergeant, ever displayed much concern for the welfare of any of the gunners on operations accomplishing what the Battery was really there for, or enough interest to contemplate paying them an occasional courtesy visit; certainly, the BSM was far too preoccupied in protecting the creases in his OGs, trimming his Ronald Colman moustache, molly-coddling the ex-Indian Army and questionably compos mentis Battery Commander, and presiding over the nightly adolescent antics in the sergeants' mess.

Apart from the opportunity to regain at least a veneer of normality by wearing civilian clothes on evening trips into town, even if only to contribute to our habitual alcoholic over-indulgence and its resultant digestive distress, or, when flat broke, bored and resentful, spending the odd, very odd, hour watching those slightly psychopathic members of BHQ staff who derived satisfaction from mercilessly teasing to distraction a couple of young local Indian transvestites who pitifully haunted the perimeter wire like over-lipsticked grotesques.

What made my temporary return to Taiping memorable, other than the fact that I developed a big crush on the young actress Roberta Haynes after watching the film 'Return to Paradise' at one of the local flea-pits, was the curious little episode of the sergeant's wife, which began when I was approached on passing the mess by one of the HQ sergeants who blurted out, "Eadie, do you know my wife?" Now, being just as aware as any other single soldier of the extramarital complications and scandals by which most married quarters in military establishments provided a welcome source of gossip, any suspected inference involving myself was bound to sound alarm bells, and left me spluttering defensively, "No, I bloody don't know your wife, Sarg, I don't even know who you are!" a response which obviously suited his mischievous intent, as he smirked with satisfaction and said, "Don't worry, son, I'm not after your neck, it's just that I've heard you come from Worksop, and so does the wife; her mother used to run a transport café on Gateford Road there," and I, breathing a sigh of relief, recalled there was at one time a poky little place crammed in-between a motorcycle agents and a hardware store run by a very large lady who had two daughters, while what came next unnerved me even more effectively than his original approach.

"How would you like to take my missus to the pictures tonight?" he offered, as if it was a perfectly normal proposal, but one which left me, sad, idealistic and unsophisticated as I was, for one of the very few times in my life struggling for an answer.

What the hell was going on! One minute I'm a broke, not exactly deliriously happy, hopefully normal little gunner, mulling over the incongruity of my latest Hollywood pin-up girl having the distinct disadvantage of apparently cinematically falling in love with Gary Cooper, who was born nearly thirty years before she was conceived, and the next minute I'm being propositioned by some barmy sergeant.

"Course I don't expect you to do it for nothing, I'll pay you; will ten dollars cover it?" Jesus, it was getting worse! I mean, all ORs recognised that most sergeants were a few rounds short of a full magazine, but this one was either abnormally desperate or just perverse! "There's a big party in the mess tonight see," he went on, as if they ever did anything else but party up there, "and I'm the organiser, but the wife wants to go to the pictures." Oh wonderful, I could just see me strolling into Taiping with a married woman, that would cause some gossip, and being well acquainted with the standard of glamour available around the married quarters, she'd probably have a face like a buffalo's backside anyway, and no amount of money was worth ending up as a laughing stock.

He was almost pleading now.

"Come on, son, will you help me out? It's just this once!" Why in God's name after all my instantaneous rationalising I answered, "Alright, Sarg, I'll do it," I'll never be entirely certain – the money perhaps? Ten dollars was after all a decent amount to a cashless gunner.

Or perhaps I was still naive enough to think I really ought to because it was a sergeant asking.

Anyway, I recklessly forgot the only piece of advice my father offered on my starting my first employment back in 1951, "Don't let anyone s--- on you," and that evening picked the lady up in a taxi from the married quarters, escorted her self-consciously into the Globe Cinema, dreading that anyone from the camp might recognise me, and crept up to the balcony to slump in my seat, hopefully unidentifiably, throughout the entire showing of the picture, the title of which to this day I fail to identify, a slight indication of continuing moral perturbation perhaps, a few mumbled answers to her references to Worksop, before crouching like Quasimodo for the National Anthem, then ferried her furtively back to her bungalow and abandoned her as quickly as possible with her baby son and the two Australians who were apparently lodging there, scarpered back to the billet increasingly and uncomfortably aware of my own unfolding small crisis of conscience, and nervously aware that I may well have just qualified as the Old Convent idiot, spent the rest of that night in a miserable mood of self-reproach.

I then awoke the next morning determinedly adamant that this was the first and definitely the last time I'd allow myself to be compromised by anyone for anything, and later that day was ordered to report to the Battery Commander's office, to be marched noisily into his presence utterly convinced I was about to be severely reprimanded for conduct unbecoming a member of the Battery, but in one of those ludicrously unpredictable coincidences, found myself instead promoted to Lance Bombardier.

Three days later, 'A' Troop trundled out of the Old Convent in convoy and headed south then due east towards the Perak River and once more approached Kuala Kangsar, there to glimpse the high minarets and huge golden dome of the Ubudiah Mosque before we crossed at the Iskandar Bridge before veering north-east to climb steadily into the hills and take up residency in a neat little ex-Malay police camp perched high above the village of Salak Bahru North to begin our second period of offensive operations.

Salak was a welcome revelation compared to our previous camp at Sungei, set at the edge of a surrounding deep strip of rubber trees beside a narrow road, its sturdily built sand-filled wooden sides and overshot corrugated iron-roofed main gate guard post overlooking any approach to the short, sharply inclined entranceway, which immediately veered right to lead alongside a compact double line of small, split door, horsebox-like accommodation units, while directly to the left of the main guard post a large black boarded building was to serve as guard room, char-wallah's shop and regular venue for our rather innocuously named 'troop nights', a morale 'keeper upper' function hastily introduced to redress the camp's complete isolation by providing a once weekly mass booze-up paid for out of the always incomprehensible finances of the troop funds.

To the rear of the OR accommodation and suitably isolated, a large colonial-style wooden pile supported bungalow provided both billet and mess for the officers, while three generously proportioned enclosed thunderbox-type toilets, a deep artesian well-fed, hand-pumped shower, and subsequent heavily protected guard posts along the east and west perimeter wire fences soon established the camp as the epitome of tropical comfort after the abysmal shortcomings of Sungei.

With nowhere in the immediate vicinity of the camp suitable as a permanent firing position, we now found ourselves compelled to venture out into the surrounding area over a range of locations to use whatever large patch of reasonably flat ground afforded us a suitable position to line up and fire whatever number of guns were needed to fire on whatever targets were offered, an arrangement which while being to us a very welcome and popular development also brought us far more into contact with the local communities and the complication of not necessarily always being appreciated, an inevitability which was certainly demonstrated at the highest level of Perak society the day we were called upon to 'take post' on a conveniently open strip of terrain near a rising bend on the usually deserted main Salak to Kuala Kangsar road and all four guns began blasting away with our usual exuberance, only for a small convoy of very smart saloon cars led by a particularly splendid example of an 1953 Rolls Royce Silver Wraith with ensign flying to come round the bend and proceed directly towards the gun position, with his Royal Highness Sultan Yusef Izzuddan Shah Ibni Alharhum Sultan Abdul Jalil Radziallan Shah, the 32nd Sultan, relaxing in the luxurious leather interior before his chauffeur, petrified by the thunderous cacophony of the four guns pounding out shells directly above his head, performed a series of alarmingly excessive deviations from his intended direction to be followed by several similar repeat performances by the drivers of the following entourage of courtiers, before eventually all regaining control and re-establishing a measure of appropriate dignity as the parade disappeared majestically into the distance, while we quietly congratulated ourselves on achieving so satisfying an effect upon so revered a personage, and continued with the perpetually thankless chore of making our small contribution towards ensuring the future of his privileged dynasty.

Later that week, either coincidentally, or perhaps in response to a note from the palace, we of Able 1 gun polished it to perfection and made a rather disingenuous display of contrition for our unfortunate display of bad timing by parking the gun on the immaculately maintained turf of the Kuala Kangsar Padang to spend a very pleasant day having our presence recorded on camera and entertaining the occasional visitor among his subjects, as we sat about and appreciated the beautiful surroundings.

It was around this time that the War Office, or the bowler-hatted coin-counters in Whitehall that controlled its finances, must have belatedly recognised that the vehicles being used by Her Britannic Majesty's armed forces in conflicts all over the globe were of the same vintage and mechanical unreliability as those used prior to the Second World War, and the first few redesigned replacements began to filter through from the UK; nothing spectacular mind you, just a few general-purpose three tonners and replacements for the ancient 15cwts, though for some debateable reason, certainly among the never impressively accomplished kamikaze-inclined drivers of 'A' Troop, this development seemed to produce an instant inability to control the more modern motors, and in a remarkably short time managed to establish a quite alarming record of reducing what were recently acquired shiny green motors to a state of near scrap, which left one Bedford QA truck deposited in a rather embarrassing position in a small ravine, a second example upside down and on top of its load of freshly cut bamboo after negotiating a slight bend, and while entering Salak Bahru camp our brand new Commer 15cwt was driven through the front wall of one of the billets, all of which hardly helped endear the drivers either to attend BHQ or REME workshops, and even less to the unfortunate gunners who spent varying periods jacked, strapped or just bedridden in BMH Taiping with numerous injuries, including one who had been unfortunate enough to be sitting writing a letter home in the billet when the Commer arrived and spent the next six months partially paralysed, finishing his National Service with a metal plate in his head.

Indeed at times, there were far too many instances within the troop when someone's incompetence, impatience and ability to self-destruct appeared far more of a threat to our safety than the fact that we were handling piles of high explosive every day in unpleasantly humid conditions, and in a climate itself capable of poisoning, inflaming or occasionally rotting away some very unexpected body parts while infesting us with hordes of alarming bugs, beetles, snakes and fevers as we chased about trying to blow up a bunch of elusive, very obstinate little Chinese dropouts creeping around the jungle, still convinced of the moral rectitude of their mission even after seven years of continual battering by a combination of up to forty thousand Commonwealth troops and the Malay Police Force.

Had anyone in a position of influence and authority had the slightest ability or inclination at that time to analyse the root cause of so many of the shortcomings evident within our little example of the British Army, it would almost certainly have proved directly related to the less than judicious standard of discipline tolerated in the Battery, but no doubt a good many, and possibly a majority of army units during that time in history were experiencing increasing difficulties when it came to sustaining the original high standards of esprit de corps, pride in a regiment and overriding sense of comradeship so diligently previously insisted upon, when the always resented inescapable necessity of National Service was being prolonged in an effort to meet the overwhelming commitments to a rapidly unwinding empire.

The fact that the numerous disparately dangerous situations were so surprisingly and equably eventually resolved says much for the innate British sense of justice and national presumption of inherited duty, at a time when young men were certainly increasingly resenting the sacrifice of two years spent far too often in some UK backwater accomplishing no more than fuelling an overriding sense of grievance, or being expected to commit themselves and quite possibly their future to being shuttled around the globe chastising some arguably entitled inhabitants who were really only intent upon achieving a comparable existence to that which they, the NS men, had seen whipped away from themselves.

Our job got done of course, and in most examples done very well, but that was due far more to the last vestiges of a traditional accedence to authority than the slightest belief that it would help enhance our increasingly tattered national standing, or was being pursued purely in the spirit of any altruistic response to a Malayan desire for autonomy, and most definitely not with any sense of conviction that we'd eventually be the recipients of even a vote of thanks for ensuring that autonomy, no matter how many times or how persuasively the politicians attempted to convince us we were the necessary perpetrators of some great moralistic obligation.

The truth of whether we were ever actually attacked by the CTs during our stay at Salak Bahru North camp, as with so many other, at the time, accepted truths, depends largely upon the degree of possibility, the reliability of the individuals who swore to its occurrence, the actual material evidence and probably the gullibility of the listener, and no doubt were it at all possible at this remove to conjure up any of the troops' former members, a hypothetical proposition which after many years of personally conducted and totally unproductive search I believe has about as much chance of success as the quest for the Holy Grail, I doubt whether the truth would in any way prove more absolute.

Certainly, there were occasions when the degree of pandemonium generated in response to what may have been perfectly explainable mistakes, misapprehensions and sheer bloody-minded mischief, suggested the total remnants of the Perak Division of the Communist MPLA had been personally ordered by the big bogeyman Chin Peng himself to eliminate 'A' Troop before the proposed Baling Peace talks at Kedah in December, but then entrusting any one of our two completely cuckoo Irish National Servicemen with anything so responsible and mentally demanding as mounting night guard, or expecting our quite demonstratively homosexual Cockney, though in truth, no one ever bothered to successfully establish his proclaimed sexual preferences, with completing more than a couple of periods in the solitary confinement of one of the camp perimeter pillboxes without eventually reaching a point where the effects of ceaselessly staring into the intimidating blackness utterly convinced him of the proximity of stealthily approaching figures, and provided an excuse for letting rip with a burst of automatic fire from the Bren gun and immediately throwing the camp into absolute mayhem with bodies flying everywhere, including some intent upon removing themselves as far away as possible from any ridiculously gung-ho suggestion of attempting to defend the camp or their companions; indeed, at times the sheer imaginative opportunism of some reluctant defenders appeared almost commendable, with one overweight technical assistant actually seen after an alarm struggling manfully to emerge from beneath an upturned trailer, an achievement which gave rise to considerable speculation as to how in the circumstances he had managed to lift and secrete himself under a piece of equipment which weighed considerably more than himself.

There was, however, at least one occasion when the alarm was raised in which the initial scepticism by the other members of the guard, which greeted a series of melodramatic-sounding moans and groans emanating from one of the pillboxes during the middle of the night, proved to be less than justified when, upon investigation by the Guard Commander, who might have been forgiven for expecting to find its occupant slumped with bullet wounds, but actually discovered him collapsed in some considerable pain from the onset of appendicitis, and which resulted in three of us making a weird and extremely unnervingly unprotected mercy dash in one of the quads to BMH Taiping.

In the often demanding pursuit of providing reasonably interesting and hopefully beneficial alternatives to occupy the infrequent days when no targets required our attention, our illustrious Troop Commander could of course never hope to satisfy everyone, but provided what he came up with appeared reasonably imaginative and not too demanding or painful, no one objected too much.

A two-day visit to Lumut's sumptuously sunshine-heated beach for a gun-pit digging contest may not, by any stretch of the imagination, have been relevant to the artillery operating requirements of Malaya, but did at least provide the winner with the prize of a large stone jar of our free issue entitlement of treacle-consistency navy rum and one more opportunity for the majority of us to get stoned senseless while enjoying the relatively unique experience of a beach barbeque, while a visit to Georgetown, Penang for a weekend away with the Australians, if perceived beforehand with a slight sense of apprehension and much scepticism as to the sort of welcome a bunch of Poms would receive, turned out to be memorably pleasant and only slightly marred by the big-mouthed obnoxious reaction of two vociferously anti-English individuals, both of whom displayed an Aussie accent which would have been more appreciated in a Glasgow shipyard and who had actually only emigrated a matter of months previously, and who were immediately told in no uncertain terms to "Belt up, you Scotch pillocks!" by one very large Queenslander; though that particular outing unfortunately resulted in our quixotically inclined No.1 spending the next few months in BMH with a severely busted knee sustained after falling into one of the deep monsoon drains in pursuit of a naval rating who had stolen a prostitute's handbag, and in consequence resulted in the questionably personally beneficial result of my promotion to full Bombardier and replacing him as No.1.

Naturally, any outing which promised even the slightest avoidance of responsibility, even if it only meant escaping the irritating insistence of lugging around personal small arms and the irritating, rash-inflicting, permanent encumbrance of waist-draped canvas bandoliers of 303 ammunition, was infinitely more appreciated than being subjected to pointlessly inappropriate exercises such as wandering out into the creepy half-light that pervaded all rubber plantations and, under the ludicrously amateur guidance and leadership of one of our Boys' Brigade inspired self-appointed jungle survival expert officers, be instructed to take up horizontal positions alongside some well-worn rubber tapper trail to spend excruciatingly uncomfortable hours lying in mock ambush, insistently silent, and being chewed, scratched, sucked and extensively and intimately physically explored by every crawly, creepy, slithery piece of bug life that existed among the damp, stinking undergrowth, and all in the interest of what? Certainly without the slightest chance of successfully surprising some CT out for an evening stroll, as had one been so stupid to venture within a mile of us, he'd have heard our clumsy efforts or probably smelt us before we had left the camp area.

Those short-statured Ulu dwellers, even if politically deluded, were professionals, not blunderingly incompetent players like us, and they could call upon an accumulation of experience gained during fourteen years of surviving and operating in that comfortless world of sunless gloom, ceaseless suspicion and habitual sensitivity to the slightest change in their environment, and would have shot us to pieces before we had a chance to lie down; no, any contemplation of mixing with that team was best left to those infantrymen or other units which at least had the benefit of some experience in Johore Bahru slogging through pukka jungle training, while we really ought to have been left to get on with doing what we were trained for and experts at, but unfortunately, there was always some egotistical fool who fancied himself as Orde Wingate or Freddie Spencer Chapman and thought he might just get a chance to go back to whatever middle-class household he came from wearing a decoration on his chest rather more significant than just the General Service Medal.

It was all so pointlessly indulgent and ridiculously inconsequential to any realistic hope of achieving anything other than an unnecessary reiteration of our appreciation of the poor bloody infantryman's lot.

We were after all exposed to considerable risks each day we spent shoving tonnes of high explosive through the guns, a fact which became only too evident with the events on 19th July 1955.

15. Causes and Effects, 1955

There were many things which could and did go wrong when operating what were only ever intended as, despite being bequeathed by the RA with a veil of moral camouflage as the 'colours' of the regiment, brutal machines with which to create death and destruction, and all artillerymen lived with the realisation that some small mistake, some disregarded precaution, some lackadaisical inconsistency, some uncontrollable, unforeseen or unexpected freak of coincidence or accident could result in catastrophic consequences.

We were of course trained perfectly adequately in how to deal with occasional mechanical misfortunes such as 'misfires', a deceptively innocuous-sounding description for something which, whenever it occurred, was capable of reducing even the most experienced of gunners to a state of momentary nervous immobility, the insignificant sounding 'click', which ominously followed the gun-layer's snatch at the small firing handle, when every man in the crew expected the great slam of successful ignition to blow the recoil reassuringly back, only to find that within the next few seconds the poor unfortunate sod who was responsible for placing the shell and cartridge into the breech now had the unenviable task of stooping over the gun-trail and, in heart-thumping dread, reach forward to gently hook the small wooden-handled wire re-cocking device onto the tiny horizontal arms of the firing mechanism before trying to pull it back into the open position, only too aware that if he failed and the firing pin slipped forward to reconnect with the soft copper percussion ring of the cartridge, three infinitely undesirable alternatives were terrifyingly possible: either the cartridge would this time successfully ignite and fire the shell, in which case he would be left with his right hand only inches above the direct line of the breech block as it instantly recoiled, or the cartridge would again fail to ignite, in which case after a third attempt to fire, the breech would have to be reopened and the defective cartridge replaced.

However, no matter how undesirable misfires may seem, to all gunners the most dreaded possibility was that of a 'premature', a term which the dictionary in its customary passionless accuracy may describe as being indicative of something happening, done, arriving or existing before the proper or usual time, but to the artilleryman simply but horrifically indicated the shell exploding within the barrel of the gun.

Questioning anything in the army at that time was just not done, at least not beyond the barrack room or beyond one's immediate circle of friends; do and don't ask, that guaranteed a more equable existence, and being as we dependably were remarkably passively acquiescent to most things thrown our way, had anyone risked the undoubted disciplinary consequences of 'appearing too nosy', any such approach would have been most unlikely to have resulted in anything approaching the actual truth.

The exact chronological order and some precise details regarding the two prematures involving both 'A' and 'B' Troops of 35 Field Battery during that awful period of July 1955 have, with the passing of over fifty years, unfortunately become increasingly difficult to ascertain, a situation not helped by the fact that, despite a considerable and continuing personal effort, no other member of both 'A' and 'B' Troops have so far emerged to establish any sort of communication.

Of course, the central obstacle to clarifying the events is the complete lack of any kind of defining information forthcoming from the military both immediately prior to the prematures and after, with even the Battery Diaries containing no more than a single entry regarding 'B' Troop premature dated 16/19th July stating 'Premature explosion of shell in barrel of gun in 'B' Troop, 1 gunner killed, 1 seriously injured, 2 with minor injuries', a regrettable situation which unnecessarily left us with no recourse other than to rely on a combination of speculation and rumour, a dilemma which produced variously diverse suppositions ranging from the ammunition having been originally buried somewhere in Malaya during the Japanese invasion in the Second World War, dumped in the South China sea after the Korean War and then fished out to be used during the Emergency, and supposedly had the fuses tampered with by enterprising CTs at the RAOC depot in Singapore, each wonderfully imaginative but with probably sufficient relativity to approach the truth, which could hardly be appreciated as to the odd little postscript which claimed that the wreckage of the two guns would be shipped back to the UK and exhibited at the Imperial War Museum.

For the 'A' Troop accident there was however no entry, although I did, by way of an ex-BHQ gunner now living in Australia, eventually come into possession of two newspaper (presumably the Straits Times) reports on the prematures, but which unfortunately gave no indication of a date for the 'A' Troop explosion and certainly no specific causes.

Meanwhile, these no doubt remain buried along with all other possibly embarrassing military information far from sight and public access in one of the deep, dark and dusty recesses of some old war office dungeon, locked, bolted and zealously guarded with the usual degree of dismissive disregard for the fact that any member of the general public who may be concerned or even entitled to peruse it, which was always so much a part of the whole ludicrous over-conspiratorially indefensible system.

The main logistical problem to emerge from the effects of the July prematures was the need to remove every round of unused ammunition from each of the gun sites and somehow transport it down to the RAOC 433 Base Ammunition Depot in Kranji, Singapore, presumably to establish what had exactly caused the accidents, although not of course before each and every individual who made up the gun crews had been assessed by practical demonstration of our ability to accomplish the job we had been doing since basic training back in Oswestry, the whole charade acted out before a major from the RAOC, a performance which we all found suspiciously questionable as to whether this was just one more instance of the powers that be attempting to direct some of the blame at the easiest target (us), and baffling as to what possible answers could be established by our self-conscious display conducted with imaginary ammunition.

As to the method of transportation for the 'bad' ammunition, we again in our naivety presumed, particularly in view of the impending Baling Peace talks scheduled for later that year, that to minimise the possibility of some enterprising band of publicity-conscious CTs attempting to extract considerable bargaining advantage by targeting the proposed movement, the most logical method of transportation would be to load it all onto a fleet of lorries and despatch them at irregular intervals to minimise the likelihood of any single calamitous interference, but no, someone decided the offending items must all arrive as one large shipment, which of course meant employing the only alternative method of transportation, the Malay Railways, a decision which led to four of us from Able 1 gun crew being detailed, accompanied by all the usual protestations and conviction of personal victimisation which accompanies the allocation of extra duties in any army, as a questionably effective guard to escort the shipment throughout its protracted journey to Singapore, an operation which, upon our arrival at the starting point of Kuala Kangsar station, immediately increased our suspicions of someone exacting some sort of vindictive satisfaction when we discovered we were to make the journey encamped in the overheated interior of a steel goods wagon coupled between two others now being loaded and stacked with the suspect ammunition by members of the Malay Regiment with all the disturbing nonchalance that seemed to be one of their not always reassuring national characteristics, while we were apparently expected to endure the depressingly discouraging prospect of a 625-mile excursion surviving on the contents of a few packs of tinned army rations, to be heated as required, and the contents of our water bottles.

Unsurprisingly, as with anything organised by the brains at 'A' Troop, no one had given a thought to anything so mundane as our comfort during the long hours of darkness and it was only during the final minutes before our departure that we managed to beg a couple of old blankets on which those of us not actually on guard could at least obtain some small degree of cushioning from the discomfort of the train's progress.

It was late afternoon when the now fully assembled train was dragged squealing and clanging and pouring clouds of smoke out onto the mainline, and we waved goodbye to a baggy shorts, grubby shirt and railway cap wearing Tamil and a few disdainful Malay and Chinese awaiting the next passenger train, and settled to the commencement of our ordeal feeling rather resentfully like rail-riding hobos in some Woody Guthrie song, not that the lush deep grasses and foliage past which we laboured at an almost walking pace bore the slightest resemblance to thundering through any part of the great plains of the American Midwest; in contrast, everything around us seemed to almost oppressively envelop our struggling progress and was only occasionally relieved by the sudden appearance of a few wire fence surrounded scattered huts and their inevitable vegetable plots, in which wizened smallholders laboured and a few excited children raced along the paths to wave enthusiastically.

We seemed to spend an eternity lounging in that sweltering steel box before we approached the first rail-side water standpipe, which at least afforded us the opportunity of taking turns to drop from our baking box to run forward and refill our water bottles, and even manage a much appreciated face splash before clambering back on-board, a routine which from then on became our usual practice whenever the opportunity arose and the only possible way we could maintain any degree of personal hygiene, the mandatory morning shave being accomplished by heating a small amount of the water on the solid fuel burner and scraping away with much evidence of blood and cursing, while being continuously buffeted and bounced while seated on the wagon floor.

This then constituted the content of our hardly exciting first few hours during the journey towards a much anticipated stop at Ipoh and the opportunity to at least view something other than continual rubber plantations and the fringes of endless stretches of deep intimidating dark forest, completely oblivious to what was about to occur next when, after negotiating a long bend in the track, the whole wagon suddenly began violently bouncing up and down and lurching sideways, with the couplings screaming in protest and almost catapulting out two of our number who were seated in the ever open doorway, a practice we had adopted, despite the fact that it obviously exposed us to any opportunistic small arms fire, in an attempt to enjoy what little cooler air was available.

A quick glance down at the wheels immediately confirmed that the wagons had left the rails and were now being dragged along the track's wooden support sleepers and with us nicely sandwiched between God knows how many tonnes of unrestrained percussive-capped high explosive.

Naturally, for the first few moments there was some confusion, as everyone initially suspected the cause may not be necessarily accidental, trains being earlier in the anti-terrorist campaign a prime target for ambush, but as everyone scrabbled around grabbing rifles and ammunition, at least we had the presence of mind to despatch one of our party through the doorway with instructions to race along the track to alert the driver, who was patently oblivious to the precarious state of his train and merrily tootling around the bend at a speed somewhere around a thankfully unimpressive ten miles an hour, and would probably have continued doing so until everything finally toppled over to spill the steel boxes of 25pdr shells across the surrounding embankment with catastrophic consequences.

Gradually, however, it became clear the message had got through as the train juddered to a complete stop, leaving the three wagons we were responsible for waving almost gracefully at an alarming angle of what seemed to be somewhere approaching the exact point of balance, while we vacated our living quarters as speedily as possible and fanned out into the undergrowth to lay ready, almost convinced we were about to be attacked at any moment.

The assault never materialised, and on reflection we realised that had it been a deliberate terrorist ambush there would be no reason for the attackers to expose themselves anyway; the damage was done, the only people who materialised being the almost distraught driver and his fireman, who were probably already contemplating accusations of incompetence and the prospect of instant unemployment, and eventually two members of the local constabulary who wandered in, one of whom accompanied our Bombardier back to his nearby kampong to alert the railway company as to what had occurred and contact our Taiping HQ regarding our predicament, but who predictably conveyed the usual lack of interest they exhibited towards any situation other than ensuring their own comfort or organising local social activities and said there was little they could do, as responsibility now lay with the railway, and left us to stand guard over the perilously unstable wagons until the decision was taken by the driver to uncouple those wagons directly in front which had avoided being derailed and drag them onto the nearest siding, leaving us to await the arrival of a black smoke belching engine propelled ancient Ransome Rapier rail crane and a gang of Indian labourers overseen by a self-important portly Sikh engineer, who bullied his gang into stabilising the ammunition wagons and with great care and much noisy communication slowly lifted each one back onto the rails before completely reloading the contents, which had apparently been so haphazardly stacked by the Malay soldiers that the load had slipped sufficiently to unbalance the wagons on the big bend.

By the time all this had been accomplished and the crane steamed back to its Ipoh depot, and the original engine and wagons returned, it was dusk, and we, who throughout it all had remained on guard, were half-eaten or stung mercilessly by bugs, soaked in sweat and just about starving, so were mightily relieved to clamber back into our hotbox to warm up some of the tinned mush which constituted most of our rations and once more continue the remaining part of our uncomfortable journey, and an hour later clanked thankfully into the big Ipoh marshalling yard to be shunted down some out-of-the-way siding for the night, which at least afforded us the opportunity to hunt down the nearest source of decent water and enjoy the first scrub down since the commencement of our travels, after which two of our number were despatched through the lines of shunted wagons to the outskirts of town, to later return with as much fresh fruit and bottles of Tiger beer as they could manage.

That night, we all slept soundly, including those detailed as guards, and next morning were literally jerked into consciousness by the sensation of once more being pushed and pulled back onto the mainline for the next and hopefully less fraught stage of our journey, which would take us down to the capital Kuala Lumpur, where we were once more shunted into a marshalling yard to bed down for the night, but which at least had the distinction of marking roughly the halfway point of our journey, and where we could again afford two more of us the privilege of setting off to restock our beer and fruit supplies before late in the afternoon of the following day continuing on towards Seremban and Tampin and the mainline junction at Gemas, before rattling down to Kluang and Johore Bahru.

The final stage saw us proceed with what seemed to us to be even less urgency than ever and entailed being shunted a couple of times to allow some enviously speedy passenger train to pass by while we grew grubbier and smellier by the hour, and true to all soldiers everywhere in any situation with which they disagreed, which would be most, we grew even more cantankerous and morose, unendingly heaping criticism and blame upon every Officer, NCO and Battery Clerk who bore the slightest responsibility for our miserable past few days, while even our first glimpse of Singapore engendered a rather less than appreciable sense of affinity with that increasingly reluctant member of the Commonwealth's diligently industrious citizens than with the numerous grey dejected faces and oddly truncated physique of captured former terrorists, which stared depressingly from inside the wire compound of Kranji jail towards the adjacent railway and its undoubtedly torturous evocation of freedom, a state of mind which was in no way decreased by the greeting and consequent treatment we received from the particularly offensive Guard Commander at the RAOC Depot guard room when we finally left the train and presented ourselves in all our accumulated grubbiness within the sanctity of his lino-lined, floor polish smelling Utopia, and who ignored, or was most probably incapable of exhibiting the slightest consideration as to the circumstances which were the cause of our unmilitary appearance, simply laid into us with all the predictable invective we had become accustomed to anticipating from anyone with an inflated presumption of his own significance.

Naturally, we all attempted, quite pointlessly, to explain, but having sufficient previous experience in dealing with the half-demented intransigence of most in his position, we eventually simply allowed him to scream and remonstrate himself to the point where even he eventually realised he was becoming rather more of an embarrassment to himself than having any satisfactory effect upon us, and concluded by instructing us to "Get your f-----g filthy disgusting bodies out of my presence, you heap of scruffy b------s, and don't let me see you again until you f-----g well bear some resemblance to f-----g soldiers!" And with these pungently pointlessly banal observations still ringing in our ears we shambled off in the direction of the unit's showers, vigorously disputing and resenting his egotistical ranting and demonstrating ourselves a far more imaginative application of the art of expletives than he could ever possibly command.

As soon as possible, we gladly vacated the depot and boarded the first available train out of Singapore's crowded station for Taiping, only to discover fate had not quite finished imposing its arbitrary interference on the equanimity of our little band when, out of the train's range of military personnel ranging from white-kneed nig-nogs on their way to join some unfortunate unit, big lazy Australians, unpretentious Gurkhas and one or two bulled-to-the-eyeball members of the RAF Regiment who littered the uncomfortable coaches, we, for some unfathomable reason, had been condemned for the duration of the up-country journey to assume duty as the train's armed guard.

16. Boh, 1955/56

After the terrible July reiteration of our physical susceptibility to unavoidable accidents, we were only too pleased to once more pack up and move on, this time into the Cameron Highlands, the area which, though very few of us appreciated it at that point, was the Malay equivalent of India's change of air stations established during the earliest days of the Raj's development to enable its administrators to escape the unrelenting heat of the lower areas by residing for a few months at the higher altitude, not that those of us who were aware of the significance were expecting to spend any time in the future lounging about, assuaged by inconspicuous punkah wallahs, or waited on hand and foot by dark-complexioned questionably obsequious servants, other than our faithful camp followers the char wallahs, and had we so deluded ourselves, any such daydreams would have been quickly obliterated by the realisation that our first night after the inconceivable slow winding ascent from the only access point at the scruffy little town of Tapah into the cloud-shrouded Highlands was to be spent under hurriedly erected tents on a despairingly inappropriate position, which during the early hours of the night was completely deluged by monsoon rains, which made even personal memories of the skin-soaked days spent on the Trawsfyndd firing range in North Wales during training back in 1954 appear insignificant and left the entire troop frantically attempting to hold onto everything we possessed before it all sailed away on the torrent that gushed through the tent lines, then disappeared among the surrounding high forest-clad hills and deep ravines, by dumping everything into any available vehicle and eventually spending the rest of the night stuffed, steaming and swearing into whatever space we could utilise on the floor of a surprisingly obliging tea-planters' double garage and succumbed to the deep sleep of the incidental, while our illustrious leaders availed themselves of the long-established class hospitality and whatever alcoholic consolation was available, before next morning, stiff and clammy, packing up and labouring the struggling lorries, quads, guns, limbers and the newly acquired great ugly armour-plated personnel carrier mounted on a Bedford truck chassis known as the Iron Pig around the unnervingly narrow precipitous bends winding through dense overhanging jungle to follow our leaders higher and deeper into the remarkably beautiful mist-laced interior of the Highlands, to eventually find ourselves at the site of what was to prove to be our last post during our time in Malaya, the sprawling Boh Tea Estate.

The estate began almost from the edge of the only road through the area before that continued on to descend a further six miles in a series of twisting bends to arrive at the single street township of Tanah Rata in the south-eastern section of the Highlands, the plantation itself stretching almost monotonously in all directions as far as the eye could see, the once luxuriant rainforest-covered slopes now flat, clad in manicured box-divided terraces of precisely planted bushes rising towards the hazy deep-blue distance on sweepingly shadowed hillsides.

The single vehicle access track to the tea factory, windingly convoluted and hacked into the fertile burnt umber soil of the hillsides, had at some point since its creation in the 1920s, where necessary, been widened and strengthened just enough for the fatalistically badly driven factory lorries to hurtle along, but was still less than suitable for excessively heavy army trucks in the hands of nervous National Service drivers, and certainly torturous enough to severely complicate its negotiation by the double-coupled quad tractors, ammunition limbers and a fifteen foot long gun we dragged apprehensively along its fragile-looking surface, led by the Troop Commander's pennant flying jeep for our introduction to the Boh Estate.

So it was with no little sense of relief that we approached the factory compound gate that first time to be saluted in by a small wizen faced, bronzed, smiling civilian Nepalese guard resplendent in a much-holed Argyle jersey and armed with an ancient shotgun, who directed our convoy to park alongside the large tea processing plant building, on what appeared to be the only available open area of any size anywhere on the man-enhanced plateau on which perched the various factory buildings and where we were instructed to dismount to await further orders, then discover inevitably that, owing to no prior arrangements having been forwarded to ensure our accommodation, the next few nights were to be spent sleeping on the floor of an empty bungalow; so having dutifully retrieved whatever kit we needed from the quad's array of exterior and interior lockers, we ferried it past the manager's large tennis court and down a precariously steep slope to where our temporary accommodation lay below the level of the factory, there to camp like burdensome refugees in one kit-littered body-strewn room, with the troop's acknowledged oddball opting to sleep among the bungalows outside supporting piles until eventually being convinced that this practice was not only hygienically unacceptable to the rest of us, but also, in view of the Cameron Highlands' rich profusion of snakes, reptiles, rats and insects, not a particularly wise choice, and we all settled into a routine requiring us to tramp up the hill every morning to scrub up and shave in a single metal trough placed in a small lean-to shed at the back of the factory, while the Troop Commander belatedly negotiated with the estate officials and an arrangement was somehow reached whereby we would erect our tent lines within the wire compound of the tennis court for the duration of our stay and no doubt involve the taxpayers back home in one more of the bafflingly ludicrous instances unique to Malaya where the military had to pay reparations to the very people who benefited most from its presence, in this case apparently for the loss of Sunday morning opportunities for some invisible manager and his aloofly absent family to maintain their exclusivity.

The gunners' and NCOs' tents, when we finally erected them, were lined up along one side of the court, a further being placed along the rear for TSM Kelly and the two troop sergeants, while the officers were accommodated in one situated at the entrance, with each tent being made that little bit more comfortable by the customary practice of raising the walls on two tiers of empty ammunition boxes, while further luxuries were the long-awaited acquisition of sprung metal beds and the provision of a shower system, courtesy of the troop's permanent member of the REME, which was built against one of the walls and utilised the factory's water supply, but which had to be almost immediately modified to include a roof when it was realised that some of the young Chinese girls who processed the tea had begun standing at one of the upper elevation windows and giggling over our daily scrubbings.

Later, a further much-appreciated and well-patronised amenity was our custom-made ramshackle tin sheet and canvas char-wallah's café erected inside the tennis court perimeter, complete with sleeping charpoys for the ever affable Mr Singh, his two large Tamil gentlemen and one Chinese boy assistant, a comprehensively stocked store area, a biscuit, chocolate, soft drinks and beer-laden counter, and a few appropriated chairs and raggedy oil-cloth covered tables, all of which created a welcome social point and belied the hut's outside appearance of something akin to the squatter shacks in Kowloon.

Obviously the only reason we had moved into the Highlands was to enable us to take advantage of its opportunities for elevated gun positions, and at Boh, high above the actual factory, was a small second plateau and it was there where it was intended three of our four 25pdrs would be set up while the fourth stayed in reserve at the lower level; herein lay our first problem, for access to the upper level was by means of a very narrow winding and extremely steep track, and our cumbersome notoriously under-powered quads, which were never designed for dealing with any terrain other than reasonably flat ground, failed ignominiously, despite numerous attempts, to negotiate the tight bends, and left us with no visible alternative other than to call in one of the six-wheeled American GMCs operated by a nearby Australian RASC unit, "Oh the utter ignominious shame of it!" at least for our always over-Blimpish officers who were noticeably absent throughout the operation, to be rescued by a characteristically laidback type who made no attempt to disguise his considerable delight in being able to put one over on a 'Pom' unit, and who to our great surprise and considerable envy actually travelled with his own supply of Fosters lager in a large ice-filled tin bath, and whose expertise made towing the guns up the hill look ridiculously easy.

The fourth gun stationed at the lower level was parked in an old lean-to shed behind the factory and directly in front of a row of three neat but basic brick and board constructed living quarters, in one of which the Nepalese main gate guard, his incredibly leathery-faced wife and one small permanently runny-nosed son lived, the neighbouring two tiny box-like cabins accommodating six young Chinese girls of varying ages who all originated from Ipoh and worked within the tea plantation factory.

The gun, which was kept in this location in the eventuality of our once more being called upon to provide a 'roving gun', a possibility never actually realised, and due as much to the limitations imposed by the Cameron Highlands' lack of suitably accessible alternative firing points as to the sheer time-consuming effort required in manoeuvring the great contraption down the road, all of which, together with the interminable need to keep the gun well maintained and in a constant state of readiness, was to be indirectly responsible for my eventual introduction to Chen Su Yin.

Su Yin was the youngest in the group of girls who first came to our notice when they began visiting the char-wallah's little shop, and naturally it didn't take long for we female company starved squaddies to begin acknowledging their presence and attempting some sort of language-complicated communication and probably even less time for our officers, who always appeared to be far more hypocritically protective of our moralistic welfare than they definitely were of their own judging by their predilection for ignoble relationships with any available wives of fellow officers, to begin questioning the situation.

Not that it bothered us unduly, we regarding it as being just one more illustration of the numerous irritating and arbitrary interferences motivated by the persistently surviving, but increasingly outdated class attitudes of the military at that time.

Eventually, however, three or four of us who were either 'Bolshy' enough to disregard the persistent 'nanny' attitude promulgated by the Troop Commander, or who perhaps were rather more susceptible to the growing effects of the 'loneliness of the long distance gunner', began to establish one of those uniquely tentative communications that relied entirely upon smiles and the odd mumbled word or two of pidgin English, which eventually resulted in Su Yin inviting me to "Ah, Tom, come sit!", an innocently charming and unexpected invitation which no doubt taxed to the limit her command of the English language and immediately removed any personal inhibitions or doubts as to the wisdom of ignoring all the official military directions regarding attempting any personal involvement with any non-European female beyond the quite hypocritically acceptable temptation to employ the services of some hygienically circumspect street girl, and accompanied by two mates I left the confines of the tennis court perimeter that evening and we made our way surreptitiously past the high civilian Sikh-manned watchtower to the small block of company accommodation and there spent a very pleasant evening enjoying the girls' very courteous and absolutely moral hospitality, consuming numerous small bowls of noodles and delicacies accompanied by pale green tea, all served on a very low table at which we three knelt awkwardly and struggled with usually hilarious, though quite surprisingly effective attempts to clumsily achieve a degree of communication sufficient to minimise our cultural differences, and in retrospect, when judged against today's unfortunate tendency to interpret any attempted boy and girl association to that of immediate crudity, the sheer artless chastity of that evening assignation at least served, if nothing else, to illustrate a depth of natural integrity which our superiors were incapable of according us.

The evening meetings continued throughout the next few weeks and my relationship with Su Yin began to develop, whether out of any great depth of genuine personal desire or simply as a consequence of being too young, too impressionable and too far from home at this remove is very difficult to realistically determine; certainly the memory of its remarkable diffidence and the fact that it at no time involved any actual physicality beyond a few chaste goodnight kisses before I clambered out of the back window to make my way undetected back to the tent lines may have added probably more to the relationship's charm and poignancy than it possibly warranted, but as to its possibilities, who can truthfully ascertain the future course of any affair of the heart? Certainly the significance of its actual innocence could never have ensured or assisted its continuation, and the certainty of its eventual demise was defined the moment its existence became apparent to our eternally unconvincingly moralistic overseers, and sure enough I soon found myself arraigned before 'Pansy Potter' and duly instructed that what appeared to me to be a perfectly innocuous, innocently artless association was in fact contrary to the propriety expected of a member of his unit, and furthermore, bordering upon a crime against my apparent Christian principles, not that these had previously in any way interfered with anything the military required of me, all of which left me begrudgingly bemused and convinced more than ever that he was incapable of appreciating and certainly determined to deter anything which to his mind may possibly affect our input to his own pathetically incompetent contribution to this obscure little war.

Of course as a result, the repercussions for me were infinitesimal when compared to the unnecessarily harsh treatment meted out to all the Chinese girls who had so good-naturedly and amicably afforded a few lonely young men an opportunity to establish a possible bond, which at least may have resulted in far more genuinely constructive effects than all the bullets and bombs achieved, but alas proved otherwise, when a couple of days later while I was on guard on the small plateau that rose above the factory and afforded an excellent bird's eye view of any activity around it, I watched with a mixture of disbelief and anger as the small group of girls were herded weeping into four taxis to be driven away and unnecessarily arbitrarily deprived of their livelihood and probably a very important contribution to their families' support.

So it was all over, and a genuinely innocent relationship was insensitively and tactlessly dismissed and no doubt blamed for the subsequent dismissals, while some guilelessly blameless individuals to whom their employment was of paramount importance were castigated purely and simply as a result of the callous indifference of individuals who were so enamoured of their own assumed importance it rendered them incapable of any sense of compassion and obviously alienated from any appreciation of the fast-approaching necessity to accept all others as an equal by the old cockeyed British abstruse mixture of conservatism and prejudice.

There were of course many other rather less disappointingly, at least to me, episodes at Boh, which predictably ran the gamut from the ludicrously irresponsible to the downright almost suicidal, and included my challenge of Lt 'Paddy' Burke while I was on guard duty and he approached obviously inebriated and demanded most objectionably to be allowed entrance without giving the required verbal identification, with the result that I most correctly threatened to shoot him, an incident which must have created a very profound effect upon him, as forever after he continually upbraided and criticised both my soldierly conduct and my effectiveness as an NCO.

There was also the strange and unresolved question of who was responsible for instigating the firing of a continual volley of rifle shots during a convoy ascent of the Highlands' torturous single-access roadway and which brought about the full investigative force of a Battery investigation and the involvement of the armies' SIB investigative branch, another time-wasting exercise which resolved nothing; after all, how do you apportion blame if someone whangs off a single round in an active service area on the pretext that he saw something suspicious from the cab of a three tonner and the rest of the convoy of twenty trucks follow suit? There was of course also the Boh and Tanah Rata Christmas, a weird and absolutely tinsel and holly devoid celebration with the opportunity to dance with some BO-smelling mate accompanied by some ancient civilian lady pianist in the gloomy lean-to shed where the fourth gun was kept, then a rocket-like ride to town in the troop jeep to get absolutely plastered on Johnny Walker before wandering in and out of the shop houses trying to encourage the poor harassed staff or some poor old backroom Cantonese ancient to risk exploding his blood pressure by drinking a totally meaningless toast with the repulsive Western hooch, then zooming back up the extremely winding road with one idiot clinging to the outside of the canvas cover, only to be catapulted off on a bend and disappear down a ravine, and finish his army career being shipped home to England partially paralysed.

Latterly, the best times at Boh were those days and nights when we'd finished despatching a few hundred tonnes of HE into the surrounding cloud-covered jungle and were able to just sit before a good fire outside the tin shack which provided overnight accommodation and, with the thin vegetable oil used in the gun's recoil system, cook piles of chips in the empty brass cartridge shell cases to be piled into thick bread slices and devoured with mess tins full of almost black Boh tea.

17. The Leaving, 1956/57

In June 1956 the extent of our time on active service in Malaya was quickly drawing to a close, and with one last bulled-up parade at Taiping HQ attended by the entire Battery, where we were all personally presented with the silver General Service Medal by a tiny little officer who was apparently Field Marshal Sir John Harding, the Chief of General Staff, we then returned to Boh to await our relief by a troop from the 48th Field Regiment, who immediately irritated us with their ill-mannered dismissal of even the most innocuous advice with regard to their future comfort and well-being, proffered in light of our past experience, so we thankfully abandoned them to their ridiculous pomposity and, having hurriedly purchased a selection of last-minute presents ranging from polished wooden elephants and tigers, a set of mahogany and brass-bound ornamental knives, which I knew my father would polish forever, one stylishly small split bamboo handbag for Lily Maud, my youngest sister, to lacquered music boxes and Japanese silkwear for the rest of the family and a gold watch for Mother and Lucy, all provided by a gift shop in Tanah Rata and delivered on our QM truck, we three days later bid a very sincere farewell to Mr Singh the char-wallah, his two Tamil assistants and Chico the Chinese boy, who all paid us the most touching and affecting acknowledgement by appearing in immaculately starched white shirts and slacks, before we withdrew down to Singapore and the Nee Soon transit camp by train and there, ecstatic at the prospect of returning home, endured, with a surprisingly good-natured and uncustomary mixture of tolerance and resignation, the usual chaotic periods of being chased about and long hours of inactivity by indulging in endless discussions of intentions and expectations on arriving home, while the tropics themselves appeared determined to contribute their own unique postscript by pouring heavier than usual monsoon downpours as we cowered under canvas before being finally crammed into lorries and delivered to the great docks to file excitedly on-board the disquietingly rusty-looking troopship, the Empire Ken.

It remains to me a mystery how nonchalantly one can dismiss so abruptly and completely the slightest nostalgic consideration for some specific juncture of our existence, and quite blatantly bid a completely unsentimental farewell to what, where or whom had previously so utterly occupied our very existence for so long a period; nostalgia came later, but that is how it was, and nothing beyond the hopefully uneventful journey down to and through the Suez Canal and home to England mattered or indeed played any part in my preoccupation, while the fact that the 80,000 British troops it had taken to guard the canal's incongruous magnificence in the past were now in the process of beating a less than dignified retreat before the relatively recent more vociferous and realistic threat of President Gamal Nasser's Russian armament supplied nationalists, really never involved or impeded our passage much more than an increase in the total number of hopelessly inaccurate empty bottles launched in our direction from the bank sides, accompanied by what, after countless repeat performances, appeared almost to be the rather unimaginative ultimate Egyptian anti-British act of defiance, the genitalia exhibition, before the eventual, far more politically destabilising nationalisation of the waterway in July incurred the catastrophic cabalistic misjudgements of Anthony Eden, the French Premier Guy Mollet and their Israeli abettors, which led to the canal's accidental blockade, and in November what would prove to be Britain's last great pretence at universal military relevance, the politically irresolute, ill-equipped, logistically inept invasion and reoccupation of the Suez Canal Zone by a morally dubious British military, which was predictably compromised by an exasperatingly ineffectual United States President Dwight D.

Eisenhower and the imperialistically hypocritical Administration directed by Secretary of State John Foster Dulles, whose mad-bull pursuit of neo-colonialistic ambitions for the USA secured an immediate withdrawal from the spineless Eden only to two years later sanction the preposterous invasion of Lebanon under no other aegis than his panic-stricken suspicion of Reds under everyone's bed, an action assisted by no other than the British government.

By the 26th of June 1956 we had passed beyond the eternally overheated Middle East and, having survived a North Sea gale during which the waves rose to an alarming height and tossed the struggling old boat with such ferocity that we were all only too effectively reminded of our vulnerability, and for two days reduced any attempted emergence above deck to the unavoidable, which involved a series of terrifying negotiations of lurching bouncing stairways, continually slamming heavy deck doors and a diet of cold hardboiled eggs and kippers in a dining area in which everything continually slid from one side to the other and the crash of falling crockery became so persistent that we were convinced we would soon be eating from the table tops, twenty-four vomit-filled hours later we were triumphantly able to gaze upon the unmistakeable white outcrop of the Isle of Wight Needles and the soft sloping downs of Alum Bay and Freshwater as we entered the dark green waters of the Solent and swung north-west into Southampton Water to berth beside the breathtakingly enormous, if increasingly redundant ocean liner Queen Mary, and find that for some unimaginable reason we could not disembark until the following day, an inconvenience which immediately provided our resident rumourmongers reason to assume the cause was Elizabeth Taylor and Richard Burton taking preference leaving from the neighbouring liner.

It was midday when we were ordered up on deck and left the ship to greet relatives and friends gathered in a small customs area, and with bear hugs and embraces take the opportunity to slip into awaiting pockets those items such as watches, rings and jewellery that we had no intention of declaring to Her Majesty's Customs and Excise during their later over-enthusiastic and never convincingly impartial kit-search conducted in one of the cavernous goods sheds, and which produced enough contraband cigarettes and tobacco to possibly affect the UK sales market, enough cheap liquor to flood the immediate area and one or two surprisingly imaginative items, such as six foot long Aboriginal blowpipes and exquisitely manufactured bamboo Japanese fly-fishing kits, before we were turned loose with travel warrants ready and dragged kit and cases onto the London-bound train, and from there each made his own arrangements for the final leg, mine being from the echoing clamour of King's Cross and a journey into a reassuringly dismissively complacent East Midlands not exactly overflowing with visible enthusiasm for the imminent publication of W S Churchill's 'History of the English Speaking Peoples', the death of Walter de la Mare or the fact that the Neutrino Particle had been discovered.

One of the curious sensations of returning home is an expectation that things will have changed during your absence, when in fact the experience unremittingly proves nothing has; certainly my homecoming produced no definable evidence of progress or improvement anywhere between London's lingering monochromatic illustration of austerity, its weary-appearing suburbs or the repetitively flat but somehow infinitely more reassuring countryside beyond, and everything was identifiably predictable, changeless, at least for the present.

Had I changed? The individual is never best qualified to judge his own possible transition and definitely not so when still only twenty-one years old; I still smoked, still drank, still swore when necessary quite monotonously, if with a greatly increased range of invective, still tended towards slightly unrealistic romanticism, still held the same beliefs, though the more negative of these had by my experiences during service become rather more extreme, particularly when it came to anything to do with authority, but then the authority I experienced at most levels had continually exhibited all the worst possible English defects.

Other than that, I was not one iota nearer to or clearer about knowing what I wanted from life, other than that I certainly could not contemplate the army as a career, so if anything I was in precisely the same mixed-up position of unrealised possible potential, unresolved capability and indefinite ambivalence as I had been at fifteen, not that any of this introspection played any part in the final short canal cut ride from Retford to Worksop resolutely sitting on my large suitcase in the guards' van like some overly protective bulldog diligently protecting its not exactly invaluable contents.

The approach into Worksop's eastern limits remained unchanged, with the high red brick presence of the Maltkins dominating the increasing spread of urban development on one side before we chugged, squealed and vibrated over the road crossing to untidily clunk to a halt beside the station's somnolent, almost deserted platforms and acrid-smelling coal smoke stained stonework, which at no time provided anything other than the most uninspiring background to any melancholic departure or expectant arrival, but nevertheless still almost redemptively provided the essential reassurance of familiarity before I departed its solemnity and passed into the soft brightness of the late June mid-afternoon sun, and directed the driver of the first available taxi to 48 Dawber Street.

On arrival home, I was then almost eaten alive by the much enlarged family dog Monty, and with the customary physically undemonstrative welcome from Mother, a much more emotional one from sister Lily Maud, and a few hours later, after my father had clomped in from his latest shift to display his so touchingly muted reaction to any positive family development by exhibiting one large smile before later displaying an almost childlike delight at the sight of the presents I had so eagerly and protectively carried home, Mother made much of showing me the ornamental dragon decorated Chinese tea service I had sent back from Hong Kong in 1955.

My two weeks of disembarkation leave, at least prior to meeting the best thing to ever happen in my life, my future and ever wife Maureen, was spent all too often wandering in and out of mustily familiar cinemas enduring crappy black and white sub-standard film noir movies involving monotonously monosyllabic private investigators or the occasional, almost treasonable Western, at least to some of the American public, which at long last indicated some overdue appreciation that the indigenous natives of the Old West probably had perfectly understandable and justifiable cause for bumping off Errol Flynn as General Custer and all the other cinematically embellished heroes in trying to protect what for generations had been their homelands, or when desperate, subjecting myself to some cinematic bubblegum concoction with predictably infantile storylines, and being no more than a showcase for some good-looking miniscule talented pop star supported by a parade of incandescently curvy teenage American beauties, before he was quite understandably relegated into obscurity and if lucky regurgitated half a century hence onto some Christmas record compilation, while the girls, in the majority, having failed to substantiate any noticeable acting abilities, disappeared into the morass of multi-channel television, and I, having subsequently found the one person who I was immediately and entirely convinced was to be the entire focus of my future, resentfully surrendered myself once more to the unutterable misery of British Railway's minimal comfort and journeyed uneventfully and unmemorably down to the khaki capital of Tidworth in Salisbury to rejoin 'A' Troop 35 Field Battery at Kiwi/Gordon Barracks, to be instantaneously hauled over the coals by my well-established nemesis Captain 'Pansy' Potter for committing the incalculable sin of failing to remove from my uniform the impressively dramatic crossed Gurkha kukri divisional shoulder flashes we wore in Malaya, a requisite which, according to him, as a two-stripe Bombardier I should have been aware of, and which achieved little more than even more resentment on my part against the whole infuriatingly detail-obsessed military and its pathetic manifestation in my own Troop Commander.

All attempts to invoke any particular recollections of the final period of my time as a soldier seem to consist of little more than a mixture of convoys out to Salisbury Plain to pursue over-emphasised, by-the-book, re-enactments of what a few months previously we had been doing far more convincingly in earnest, mind-numbingly freezing morning periods of delivering rock-hard coal to the married quarters, an occasional, invariably false alarm IRA attack, the occasional light relief when some clown superficially shot himself into BMH or attempted to steal the NAAFI till takings, or when drunk avoiding the traditional Salisbury honey traps where a couple of young females would try to entice any soldier down an alley to be kicked to hell by the awaiting local gutless wonders.

Of course, the greatest concern of those in my position was the developing possibility of being denied our demobilisation and being pushed into the swelling ranks of those unfortunates being included in the build-up to the proposed invasion of Suez, but thankfully, I was spared and so it ground on, with me fighting hard to remain committed and the military as usual never entirely or visibly being satisfied with the degree of anyone's commitment.

Relievedly, all things must end, and three years to the day, and having made my goodbyes to those of my old pals who were still with the troop, and effortlessly resisting the Regimental Commanding Officer's laughably insincere attempt to induce me to extend my active service with the guarantee of a third stripe (I would remain on reserve for a further four years), I made my final journey homeward and found, rather disappointingly, that all my effort, contribution and diligence had been summarily dismissed in my record of service, most probably at 'Pansy' Potter's recommendation, by the single description of "Not a particularly effective NCO".

So passed some of what are generally regarded as among the most formative years of any young man's life, as with the majority of young males of that era without achieving any profound revelations regarding either the meaning or even understanding of life, or indeed any enlightening vision, indication or illumination of how its experiences may affect our future, or even what that future might be.

Was any part of it of any particular worth in terms of improving any aspects of our development as members of society, or did little of it actually play any lasting role in how we developed? I would certainly question whether it necessarily produced many answers to society's ills, the actual root causes of such problems hold far more indications as to possible effective preventative or remedial measures than any strictly militaristic, overly disciplinarian, proposals could ever achieve.

It could in fact be quite validly argued that such an approach would, when applied to the majority of today's sceptical youth, cause far more problems than it could possibly hope to address, while the one consideration those who propose this outdated cure conveniently disregard is that not only is the reintroducing of any type of National Service now so completely unworkable logistically, but that even the military brass themselves reject it, the prospect of attempting to confront modern emergencies by reintroducing the same set of problems that existed fifty years ago, when the military continually struggled to produce a disciplined and reliably effective force from an over-abundance of resentful personnel and a lack of half-decent equipment even at a time when such attributes as loyalty, conformity and parental influence were far more established and appreciated, hardly indicates any possibility of future success.

Far better surely to continue dealing with those modern problems which so often resist all attempts at non-violent solution by persisting with the system whereby those who voluntarily enlist at least presumably recognise that a military career will almost inevitably at some stage require them to engage in hostilities, some of which may well involve situations demanding an even greater degree of discipline and self-reliance than those faced by the previously conscripted army.

Naturally, I can only comment on how the actual experience of military service affected me as an individual at the time I was involved, and as far as I was concerned, reiterating an already appreciated recognition that no plum-laden accent, university education, public school grounding or privilege denoted the slightest indication of common sense or imagination, or helped instil any conviction or reassurance that those who enjoyed their traditional benefits were anything other than just as capable of committing the most profound mistakes and misjudgements as any lesser member of society, and therefore to me indicates that one's own aberrations are far more acceptable whatever the consequences.

Nor did my experience necessarily reveal any great enlightenment as to how I ought to conduct myself or how I should present myself to the greater world, which thank God was already previously instilled within my character by a combination of genetic endowment and positive parental influence, a mixture which to my mind contains a far more effective defence against any possible social misdemeanours than any belated reintroduction of largely oppressive disciplines or even organised interference.

While some misinformed or deluded individuals continually refer to the assumed benefits accrued from National Service such as the increased opportunities to communicate with other social classes, as if this alone could be a guarantee of diffusing class differences and adjusting the status quo, in my experience it actually resulted in no more than a continual, and at times even more extensive reiteration of our historically established differences and prejudices, and left most of those who served with me with a conviction that little in our entrenched social divisions would ever realistically undergo anything other than certain superficial changes no matter how many times the differences were thrown together.

Naturally, my service brought with it some benefits, comradeship yes, though even that actually proved to be transient, and despite considerable effort continually resisted most attempts to re-establish even the most tenuous contacts.

To me, the one and uniquely definitive experience of travel proved without doubt to be the best and most appreciated by-product of military service, though despite its wonderful opportunity to gain access to other cultures, I can claim no resulting ambition to extend my travels further than a few hardly enlightening trips to Belgium, Switzerland, France and Spain, or indeed any realistic desire to return to the Far East, for there would, to my mind, be little point, believing as I do that what we saw and when we saw it was both unrepeatable and irreplaceable; we were without doubt entirely privileged in so many ways, from the incredibly affecting adventurous experience of spending a so long and so leisurely period at sea in a situation of quite acceptable indications of military discipline, experiencing previously undreamt-of locations, while each still presented a far more varied and inimitable representation of its cultural disparity, and before most discarded such contrasts and capitulated into the vulgarly inappropriate counterfeit copies of American architectural influences and embraced far too avidly Western cultural inclinations.

I still much prefer to retain memories of those fantastic opportunities to interact with those of my own age group on that unstable old steamer than attempt to subvert them with any contemplated luxury-filled excursion on today's vast cruise leviathans or be forced to endure the computer-decreed minimally required personal space in some airborne cylinder, no matter how padded, much as I prefer to recall experiencing life in the Crown Colony of Hong Kong before all trace of that indefinable atmosphere generated by being in the mysterious east was obliterated by the glitzy, gaudy, maniacally competitive proliferation of malls, tunnels, overhead highways and the ever-changing vertically fixated, vulgarly neon-clustered corporative glass blocks regrettably camouflaging what once gave the colony its inimitable identity to such an extent that what was once the norm has now to be sought out as a tourist oddity, as is the case with modern Far Eastern cities from Singapore to Shanghai.

Postscript:

In 1958 I married Maureen, whom I had known from the age of fifteen.

In 1962 my elder brother Oliver Charles contracted tubercular meningitis after sustaining damage to a knee in a colliery accident and died in Newstead Abbey Sanatorium on 27th August.

He was 42 years old.

On 28th January 1964 my father died in Nottingham General Hospital as a result of the increasing debilitating effects of pneumoconiosis.

He was 64 years old.

My mother died on 11th January 1970 of a haemorrhage and hypertension.

She was 70 years old.

My eldest sister Lucy Florence died in April 1980 on the Isle of Wight of a haemorrhage and hypertension.

She was 56 years old.

My brother Bert Alan died on 30th December 1988 of heart failure.

He was 58 years old.